Sheringtons

A History

Geoffrey Edgar Sherington and
Bruce Banfield Sherington

DARLINGTON PRESS

First published in 2014 by Sydney University Press

Sydney University Press
Fisher Library F03
University of Sydney NSW 2006
AUSTRALIA
Email: sup.info@sydney.edu.au

National Library of Australia Cataloguing-in-Publication Data

Author:	Sherington, Geoffrey, author.
Other Authors/ Contributors:	Sherington, Bruce Banfield, author.
Title:	Sheringtons: a history / Geoffrey Edgar Sherington, Bruce Banfield Sherington.
ISBN:	9781921364570 (paperback)
Notes:	Includes bibliographical references.
Subjects:	Sherington family.
	Immigrants--Australia--Biography.
	British--Australia--Biography.
	Australia--Emigration and immigration--History.
	Great Britain--Emigration and immigration--History.
	Australia--Genealogy.
	Great Britain--Genealogy.
Dewey Number:	929.20994

Cover image from front advertisement in Oliver Trickett, *Guide to the Jenolan Caves, New South Wales* (Sydney: WA Gullick, Government Printer, 1922)

Cover design by Miguel Yamin

In memory of William George Sherington
(1907–1993)

Contents

Foreword vii

I Suffolk: The Land of the South Folk 1
II South London and Beyond 61
III Sydney: The Globite Story 123

Appendix I Family Line of Descent 191
Appendix II Family Biographies 193

Foreword

In the digital age the search for one's ancestors is a popular pastime. It has even become a form of televised entertainment with celebrities on such shows as *Who Do You Think You Are* seeking the aid of historians and other experts on their family origins. Some hope that with the click of a mouse, a long-lost file will be located and details of ancestors will come to life on the screen. And with the advent of digitised archives it is also now possible to link transnational records to give snaps of individual and families at points in time.

What is now known as 'family history' originated from the study of genealogy designed to reveal the history of the 'family name' through the male line of descent. Using the census data in Britain and the United States, such organisations as ancestry.com can produce booklets on family names. Thus we can learn that at the census of 1851 in Britain the name of Sherington was recorded for only fifty-seven individuals of whom more than half resided in Lancashire. By 1881, there were thirty-nine Sheringtons by name throughout Lancashire, Durham and Yorkshire, nine in London and seven in Warwickshire. And by then there were also small pockets of Sheringtons in North America, particularly in Michigan.[1]

Despite the new digital era helping to identify the locality of nineteenth-century and even present-day families, the extended genealogy of family names remains often uncertain, particularly in locating the connections between place and names. Inherited family names, traditionally through the male line of descent, emerged in the British context as surnames or additional second names. In the Anglo-Saxon era there were often just single personal names. Following the Norman conquest of Britain surnames emerged in the medieval period, although only occasionally did medieval surnames become hereditary. Until the creation of parish registers and the universal recording of births, marriages and deaths, the spelling of surnames varied and individuals often had more than one surname. Modern forms of surnames came from the phonetic spelling of names usually found in the parish registers of the seventeenth or eighteenth centuries.[2]

Surnames which then merged into family names had various origins. The most popular form was related to locality.[3] The name of Sherington originally referred to a locality being Anglo-Saxon in origin. In Old English, Sherington was *Sciringtun* meaning Scira's farm or settlement. Who Scira was is now lost in time but the name survived. In Buckinghamshire, near Newton Pagnell, there is the village of Sherington dating from a seventh century Anglo-Saxon settlement. The American historian A.C. Chibnall, tracing his own family history, produced a 1960s study of this village of Sherington with a focus on land and land holdings from before the Norman Conquest until the twentieth century.[4]

---

1 *The Sherington Name in History* (Provo: The Generations Network, 2007), 39, 64 and 68.

2 P.H. Reaney, *A Dictionary of British Surnames* (London: Routledge and Kegan Paul, 1976), xii–xiv.

3 Ibid., xiv–xvii.

4 A.C. Chibnall, *Sherington: Fiefs and Fields of a Buckinghamshire Village* (Cambridge: Cambridge University Press, 1965).

This Buckinghamshire village may have been the first place in England to be named 'Sherington' and certainly members of this Sherington line as well as others have continued to visit it as a 'homeland'. By the fifteenth century, however, there were other places associated with the name of 'Sherington' sometimes now spelt 'Sherrington' or even 'Sharington'. These included villages in Warwickshire and Wiltshire as well as Norfolk where 'The two most common place name suffixes are the old English *ham*, usually translated as "village or settlement"; *tun*, settlement or farm'.[5]

About one-fifth of the sixteenth-century surnames in Norfolk were derived from local place names, less than the national average of about one-third but still significant. Many of those in sixteenth-century Norfolk with 'locality' surnames derived these from the neighbouring County of Suffolk, and particularly from East Suffolk.[6] The inter-connection between Norfolk and Suffolk is also an important part of the story of this line of the Sherington family which is the focus of this book. Parish and other records suggest that since the sixteenth century this particular family has spelt its surname with an 'e' and one 'r'.

Genealogy was thus an important foundation of this history which has taken a half a century to research and compile, involving more than one generation of the extended Sherington family in Australia as well as cousins in Britain. Beginning before the digital age, research first concentrated on extensive parish records in Suffolk as well as family papers and official births and death records from London and then family papers and records in Australia. With the coming of the global age of communications, contact was re-established between the descendants of the Pretty family from Ipswich and the Sherington family of Upper Norwood near the former Crystal Palace in South London. The

5 Tom Williamson, *The Origins of Norfolk* (Manchester: Manchester University Press, 1993), 85.

6 R.A. McKinley, *Norfolk Surnames in the Sixteenth Century*, Department of English Local History, occasional papers, second series, no. 2 (Leicester: Leicester University Press, 1969), 17, 25.

Pretty–Sherington marriage alliance in the nineteenth century provided a focus as did the Sheringtons who left London for Australia and America. Indeed this recent research clearly revealed how the digital age can actually reunite extended families in a new bond of friendship.

But understanding the history of a family involves more than genealogy. In recent decades historians have come to understand the history of the family in terms of its changing structure, values and contexts. Age and gender relations in particular have become crucial as part of the history of the western family. This history tries to understand the changing contexts of one particular line of the Sherington family over almost five centuries. As is the case with most histories, this is a narrative of change which draws upon a variety of sources to try to grasp the process which led to migration from Suffolk into London and then to Australia and also to the Americas. As such it tries to provide some understanding of the changing meaning of 'family' as well as wider social and economic contexts from the sixteenth century onwards set within three specific localities – the village of Westleton in Suffolk, South London and Sydney, New South Wales.

This is therefore not so much just the history of 'a family' but of many families over time. The family name of Sherington provides a link to those born with this name, or associated through marriage or in other ways. There is also a specific focus on the idea of enterprise. It is now fashionable to concentrate on the cultural aspects of the family exemplified through love, marriage and the upbringing of children. These are present in this history, but principally this is an historical study of the middling ranks of society where the survival of the family depended on not so much personal attachments but varying fortunes and enterprise. For most of these centuries the family was an economic enterprise as much as a form of emotional attachment. In Suffolk there was the family farm; in South London a family business based on the new world of retail and consumption; and in Sydney the family manufacturing firm of Ford Sherington. Economic fortunes of the family thus governed the lives of most of the family members. Indeed we see here the creation of the family business, which has been so important in middle-class social and economic life for most of the recent past.

Research for this book has been an extended family affair, taking place over half a century and involving extensive effort and cost, both financial and personal. In particular we would like to thank our father, William George Sherington (to whom the book is dedicated), our Australian-born cousins Charles Richard Sherington and Dorothy Barbara Dawson, and our English cousin Mark Shephard who has revealed to our generation what was unknown to our Australian-born fathers' and mothers' generation. Our brother David generously funded the cost of the production of the book.

Outside the immediate family others have assisted in many ways. Our long-time English friends William Fullick and Margaret Byrne were assiduous in their research of aspects of the Banfields and Sheringtons in nineteenth-century South London. In a recent bike-ride our old Australian friend Ross Hayward visited and took photos of Middletown in California where a member of the Sherington family was murdered in 1890. Others have contributed, not the least, through research assistance or by reading and commenting on the text. They include Joanna Martin, Roger Kennell, Dick Selleck, David Carment, and Julia Horne. Thanks are also due to Susan Murray-Smith, Agata Mrva-Montoya and Bronwyn O'Reilly of Sydney University Press for producing this history. For all of the above we thank you.

Many of the sources for this history are still held in private possession. It is hoped that in future most of these will be deposited in the Mitchell Library, Sydney.

This history is extensive and ambitious in its breadth. It commences in the Anglo-Saxon past and virtually ends at the time the Sydney Opera House was being completed in the early 1970s. My late brother and I hoped that it will reveal something of the lives and experiences of our ancestors. And perhaps future generations will carry this history into the twenty-first century.

One final word on nomenclature. As with many families of English heritage, the name of William was often given to the first-born son. However, from the nineteenth century there was often a second personal name attached. To distinguish so many Williams this practice of including a second personal name is used in the latter parts of the text.

Geoffrey Sherington
Sydney
October 2013

I

Suffolk: The Land of the South Folk

Between the wide, weathered scenes of Norfolk, held back by long winters and late springs, and the more infiltrated country of Essex, one soon comes to recognise and identify a landscape of cornfields, scattered farms and villages and flint-towered medieval churches. Many of its farmhouses and churches face up to the cold winters of winter and springtime that blow over the North Sea and across marshes and heaths and clay plateaux, but usually they have been found some shelter in the depth of a small valley of willows or a fold in the clay. The distinctiveness, rather hidden, secluded personality of these lands, that stretch fifty miles from the Cambridgeshire fens to the eastern shingle shores, derives most from its makers. It is primarily the landscape of the South Folk, the English of southern East Anglia: Suffolk.

Norman Scarfe, *The Suffolk Landscape*
(London: Hodder and Stoughton, 1972), 23.

East Anglia

Sheringtons were long attached to the county of Suffolk on the east coast of England. In the recent past, such attachments have even helped to reveal the Anglo-Saxon past of East Anglia of which Suffolk forms an integral part along with the neighbouring county of Norfolk. This history thus begins with a mid-twentieth century discovery of the Anglo-Saxon past before returning to the history of East Anglia.

In the English summer of 1938, Edith Pretty, widow of Frank Pretty, decided to excavate a number of mounds that were in the grounds of their estate at Sutton Hoo near Woodbridge Suffolk. Ever since Frank and Edith had purchased the property in the 1920s they had been fascinated by the size and nature of these mounds, one of which had been dug up in the nineteenth century. In 1932, Edith herself had attempted further work. Now she sought the assistance of the British Museum and was directed to a local farmer Basil Brown who undertook casual archaeological work.[1]

In June and July 1938 a number of trenches were excavated, revealing many items. Brown then discovered a number of ship rivets, and ultimately the outline of a large ship's hull in the sandy soil typical of East Suffolk. After three mounds had been cleared work was suspended having already attracted much local attention. The following summer of 1939, with the war approaching, Brown returned to complete his work.[2]

The Pretty family had been related by marriage to the Sheringtons from the late nineteenth century. This prewar archaeological dig now provided a symbolic link to both Suffolk and the extended Sherington family, many of whom are now located in

---

1 Mary Skelcher and Chris Durrant, *Edith Pretty: From Socialite to Sutton Hoo* (Leiston: Leiston Press, 2006), 51–52. For a fictional account of these events, see John Preston, *The Dig* (London: Viking, 2007).

2 Angela Care Evans, *The Sutton Hoo Burial Ship* (London: Trustees for British Museum, 1986), 12–22.

Sydney. In the summer of 1939, Olive Sherington, wife of Arthur Sherington who had come to Australia with his two brothers in 1889, was on the Sutton Hoo estate, renewing a twenty-year friendship with Edith Pretty whose husband Frank had also been a lifelong friend of Arthur. Her presence at the discovery was later recorded in the Australian press in what was described as an 'exclusive story' about human remains in the burial mounds on the Pretty estate. Obviously eager to appear in the Australian media, Olive sought to discount rumours that the body was that of a sixth-century Anglo-Saxon King:

> I do not believe that the remains are those of King Raewald who leaned to Christianity . . . the Burial was typically pagan and unchristian. I spent a week watching the searchers working with infinite caution using a fine brush and tiny probe. I was astounded when they discovered that modern fashion had not bettered those of 600 AD.[3]

In Britain, the national media and others soon became interested. While Brown continued to excavate, the British Museum intervened and took over much of the work to prevent damage to any archaeological objects. In effect, many items of priceless treasure were found in the remnants of the ship. By the end of July the treasures had been sent off to the British Museum and a team from the Science Museum had been brought to survey the ship's remains. In August 1939, a Treasury Trove inquest was held at the local parish hall, concluding that the treasures came from the burial of 'an important person' of 1300 years previous when the nation state of England did not even exist. After some consideration, Mrs Pretty, the formal owner of the so-called million-pound grave decided to give all the treasure to the British Museum, the most generous single-person lifetime gift the museum had ever received.[4]

---

3 *Daily News* (Perth), 5 August 1939, 3.

Despite the views of Olive Sherington, some already confidently suspected who had been in the burial ship. The Anglo-Saxon scholar, Munro Chadwick of Clare College Cambridge, wrote in June 1940 that it was definitely Raedwald, king of the East Angeles and member of the Wuffingas dynasty (with 'Wulfigas' meaning the offspring of the wolf) which probably originated from Scandanavia but had come to dominate the kingdom of East Anglia which spread throughout the region of present day Suffolk and Norfolk. Raedwald had converted to Christianity but had later recanted before he died in 624 or 625 AD. The burial ship was thus the resting place of a warrior king, prepared for death and buried in full battle regalia. Half a century of research on the objects within the site have confirmed both the identity of Raedwald and the importance of this archaeological discovery. Sutton Hoo is now seen as a site of world significance, not just of the Anglo-Saxon era, but of pre-medieval Europe. The objects within the grave mound reveal a material culture, with links to both Northern Europe and the Mediterranean, as well as representing symbols and protocols of Anglo-Saxon kingship.[5]

The early history of Suffolk lies at the heart of the ancient past of England. Archaeological evidence has long established that there were 'early agriculturalists' as settlers from at least 3000 AD but perhaps 'hunter fishers' from 6000 AD who had arrived from Europe.[6] The areas which became East Anglia were once the home of the Iceni and 'Queen' Boudica who rose up against the Romans in 60 AD. And when that revolt was put down the Romans turned to building towns, roads and forts as

---

4 Martin Carver, *Sutton Hoo: Burial Ground of King's* (London: British Museum Press, 1998), 2–24.

5 Evans, *The Sutton Hoo Burial Ship*; Peter Warner, *The Origins of Suffolk* (Manchester: Manchester University Press, 1996), 70–93; Tom Williamson, *The Origins of Norfolk* (Manchester: Manchester University Press, 1993), 72–83; Carver, *Sutton Hoo*.

6 Norman Scarfe, *The Suffolk Landscape* (Chichester: Phillimore, 2002), 47.

well as individual farms, the imprint of which still remains on the Suffolk landscape. The Roman departure at the beginning of the fifth century left the way open for new settlers from across the North Sea.[7] Coming from Germany, of Anglian, Saxon and Frisian origin, new settlements along the east coast of England appeared in the fifth century AD. Despite earlier views that this was an Anglo-Saxon 'invasion', the new settlers probably did not so much exterminate or even eliminate earlier settlers as absorb them and even use earlier places of settlement. They soon left the coast and penetrated inland.

The new settlers soon became part of an English Christian civilisation in the British Isles. When the Church scholar Bede composed *A History of the English Church and People* in 731 AD there were already clear signs of the foundations of an English language and English customs. A loose set of kingdoms emerged which some now even see as forming the basis for an English nation under King Arthur (who translated Bede's history into early English) and later King Harold whose reign over other Anglo-Saxon kingdoms was brought into being by threats from the Danish Vikings and then the Norman French.[8]

From the outset it seems that the Anglo-Saxons lived within family units as part of small communities with a mixed farming economy of crops and livestock. By the late sixth century such settlements were even trading in jewellery, glassware and pottery with not only Scandinavia but with the Mediterranean. Much knowledge has come from burial sites such as Sutton Hoo which has reinforced the view of wealth and power as well as contacts into Europe of the East Anglian dynasty of the Wuffingas. The seventh century when Raedwald ruled was also the period of great change with the advent of Christianity, the development of

---

7 Peter Warner, *The Origins of Suffolk*, 29–60.

8 Bede, *A History of the English Church and People* (London: Penguin, 1955 [731]); Geoffrey Hindley, *The Anglo-Saxons: The Beginnings of the English Nation* (London: Robinson, 2006).

the nearby town of Ipswich as a trading centre with the Rhineland, and the abandonment of old settlements and the establishment of new ones. An extensive network of local villages in East Anglia was created in the four centuries before the Norman invasion of 1066.[9]

It is also from the Anglo-Saxon period that the idea of 'Suffolk' emerges even though the name itself is not recorded in a document until c.1045. The term applied to those 'folk' who lived at the southern boundary of the kingdom of the East Angles. The boundaries of this 'folk area' was divided by a major double valley to the North – Waveney and Little Ouse dividing the South Folk from the North Folk (Norfolk) – while the River Stour divided them both from the kingdom of Essex, the East Saxons. What reinforced these territorial divisions were administrative and ecclesiastical forms of Church governance.[10]

Once themselves invaders, Anglo-Saxons were also conquered. Prior to the Normans, the Danes crossed the North Sea to raid Britain, landing in East Anglia (865–879). The new Danish settlers seemed to have encouraged trade at Ipswich and assisted the creation of market towns. At the same time, Christianity flourished. The first bishop's see was probably established at Dunwich on the Suffolk coast in the 630s. There were also a number of monasteries founded in the seventh century onwards. And by the Domesday survey of 1086 there were 400 churches in Suffolk, although most were probably built of timber with stone probably not much in use until the tenth century.

The Anglo-Saxon period also brought into being a form of administration and governance that would persist beyond the Norman invasion and into the Medieval period. Again this was based on an idea of 'family'. The division of Suffolk into 'hun-

---

9 Warner, *The Origins of Suffolk*, 60–107.

10 David Dymond and Peter Northeast, *A History of Suffolk* (Chichester: Phillimore, 1995), 38; Williamson, *The Origins of Norfolk*, 82–83.

dreds' dated from at least the tenth century. Originally representing a hundred *hides* or family holdings, there were twenty-five hundreds in Suffolk at the Domesday Book survey in 1086. Most took their names from the original open-air meetings of their Anglo-Saxon courts. The hundred became the basis of all public administration in medieval England, judicial, fiscal and military.[11]

The nature of this settlement gave rise to social patterns which persisted beyond the Norman conquest. Much of the population in pre-1066 East Anglia lived on the land as freemen (*creols*), or bondmen owing service to a lord. The Domesday Book estimated that about forty per cent of the population in Suffolk were freemen. In comparison, the proportion of freemen throughout out England was only fourteen per cent. But freedom was gendered with freewomen being less than two per cent in East Anglia. Even then, no man was 'lordless' with the chosen lord of a freeman being usually the King, Queen, Earl, bishop or someone from the seigniorial class (*theng*). Most of these freemen were composed of mixed ethnic background, including descendants of recent Danish migration, and comprised three groups: the *theng* who had extensive holdings; a 'middle class' who often held shared land holdings and included significantly many kinship groups who were involved in church building and land holding; and finally those numerous humble freemen who held very small holdings.[12] The 'peculiarities' of East Anglia, and the significance of 'free' families and 'middling ranks' of society were thus well established at the end of the period of Anglo-Saxon England.

The Norman conquest brought a new division of the land. The *theng* or seigniorial class virtually disappeared in the distribution of spoils. By 1086, the Domesday Book revealed seventy-

---

11 Warner, *The Origins of Suffolk*, 118–19, 145–47; Dymond and Northeast, *A History of Suffolk*, 18.
12 Warner, *The Origins of Suffolk*, 182–84, 195–203.

one 'tenants-in-chief' in Suffolk (some of whom also held lands in Norfolk and Essex). Very few were English in background; the vast majority were Norman-French. The landholders included the King, but also barons and earls. The Normans also favoured the Church, and abbeys and monasteries became property holders. The symbols of the conquest became the castles now built throughout the Norfolk and Suffolk countryside.[13] The Normans also brought their own language while new personal names such as Geoffrey, Robert, Thomas and William soon became accepted.

The conquest was not so much a dramatic break in English history as the 'take-over by yet another dynasty and aristocracy, amounting to less than 5000 people, while beneath them English society, survived relatively unchanged'.[14] By the thirteenth century, Suffolk was becoming a place of prosperity. There was a growing population, a demand for food, and rising agricultural prices. Both landholders and tenants responded by improving rural productivity. There was also expansion in domestic industry, crafts and retailing. In each 'manor' the lord had his 'hall' or courthouse, based on the 'hundred' which became the administrative heart of the community. He or his bailiff, cultivated the 'demesne', the home farm which surrounded the hall, being enclosed in hedged fields and sometimes intermixed with the lands of his tenants. Many lords had other 'privileges' over windmills, church parishes and even the gallows. Increasingly, the manor was no longer equivalent to the parish with many manors being divided up into multiple forms.[15]

From the thirteenth century Suffolk became rather different from Norfolk, its northern neighbour. Both Suffolk and Norfolk had long been tied together by a common environment and topography along the North Sea coast. Even in the twentieth century both counties were seen as sharing a common environmen-

---

13 Dymond and Northeast, *A History of Suffolk*, 35–38.
14 Ibid., 35.
15 Ibid., 42.

tal heritage – low flat 'broads' marked by rivers flowing to the coast with coastal high grounds washed away by the sea over centuries.[16]

Until the Norman invasion both Norfolk and Suffolk also shared a similar social structure of many free small landholders. The idea and even the reality of the independent free holder survived but increasingly in Norfolk, 'a society of essentially small-scale producers was gradually replaced by one with a more polarised tenurial and social structure'.[17] In Norfolk large landholders and the monarchy came to own one-third of the manors, although most of the population was along coast still sharing ties and even common ties with neighbours to the south in Suffolk.[18]

In Suffolk the largest medieval landholder was the Church with many smaller landlords particularly in East Suffolk. Increasingly, freemen and tenants in Suffolk came to farm small holdings. Tenants used their land intensively. Much land was in open fields but there were also farming in pasture, hay-meadows, marshes, fens, commons and woods. Many holdings were less than one acre. The rules of inheritance could lead to the break-up of family holdings; the basic farm units once called 'tenements' were soon highly fragmented and tenants came to hold land across many different tenements. In return for their land, tenants were expected to do labour services for their lord or give money in lieu. Labour obligations were various including ploughing, carting, threshing and cleaning ditches and thatching. But medieval Suffolk was hardly bound by any form of serfdom with tenants tied to the land. Many moved outside their local village travelling for up to thirty miles to a new house. The turnover of population associated with the local manor could be dramatic even in the space of five years.[19]

---

16 A. Heaton Cooper and W.G. Clarke, *Norfolk and Suffolk* (London: A. and C. Black, 1921).
17 Tom Williamson, *The Origins of Norfolk*, 3.
18 Susanna Wade Martins, *A History of Norfolk* (Chichester: Phillimore, 1997), 31–50.

Social changes as well as shifts in patterns of land ownership began to re-shape the Suffolk countryside. First, there was growing social and political unrest during the fourteenth century often directed against large landowners such as the abbeys. In 1325 such unrest led to the deposition and death of Edward II. In 1349, the bubonic plague from Europe brought the Black Death wiping out, in the space of a few months, up to half the population of about 250 000. The plague left a legacy of uncertainty over land tenure and obligations. The King and many of the landowners sought to re-assert their traditional rights over the common labourers who were now emboldened by the contexts of a shortage of labour following the plague. In 1381 the 'peasants' revolt' was directed generally against the ruling class. De-population in the 1300s, associated partly but not entirely with the effects of the Black Death, then led to the decline of tenancies and vacancies of holdings. As a result, many lords came to lease out their demesne land as a way of raising cash. Many former small-farm tenants now became substantial large landholders through land transfers and consolidation.[20]

By the eve of the sixteenth century Suffolk was being transformed. New opportunities and specialisations had emerged, changing the older landscape of arable crop farming. East Suffolk along the coast had an economy based on cows, dairy, butter and cheese, and leather. Most land holdings were still only ten acres but some were being consolidated into forty-acre farms. In 1300, Suffolk had lagged behind Norfolk in terms of large urban centres and the intensity of arable farming. By 1500 Norfolk was losing ground to the economic development of Suffolk which had developed pastures and a textile industry which surpassed its northern neighbour.[21]

---

19 Mark Bailey, *Medieval Suffolk* (Woodbridge: Boydell Press, 2007), 10–89. See also Dymond and Northeast, *A History of Suffolk*, 41–44.

20 Bailey, *Medieval Suffolk*, 242–63; John Hatcher, *The Black Death: The Intimate Story of a Village in Crisis 1345–1349* (London: Phoenix, 2009).

21 Bailey, *Medieval Suffolk*, 290–306.

There was also new wealth. In 1327 fewer than thirty parishes in Suffolk had just one individual who paid thirty per cent or more of the total tax paid; by 1524, there were 180 parishes where this occurred. Wealthy individuals tended to dominate where parishes were low in acreage. There were also other changes between the different regions, with the once-dominant agricultural 'high Suffolk' of the mid parts of the county giving way to the emergent south-west where a new cloth trade was located. And in-between were such parishes as those along the coast where foreign trade, fishing and boat building had produced new opportunities.[22]

Throughout rural England, a changed social structure had emerged. At the top was the aristocracy, generally with inherited titles, then the gentry, just below the nobility in status and birth, and emerging was the new class of farmers known as 'yeomen'. Origins of the yeomen lay in being 'free' tenant holders; their social position differentiated them from the mass of 'peasants' or 'villiens' who were still bound to the lord of manor by custom and service. Some yeomen even sought a status bordering on the gentry. As such they formed a substantial part of the middle ranks of medieval society, now free but ready to serve King and country in war and peace:

> They were a substantial rural middle class whose chief concern was with the land and agricultural interests, a group that lived 'in the temperate zone betwixt greatness and want,' serving England, as it 'was given a middle people . . . in conditions between the gentry and the peasantry' to serve.[23]

22 Hilary Todd and David Dymond, 'Population Densities, 1327 and 1524' in David Dymond and Edward Martin (eds), *An Historical Atlas of Suffolk* (Ipswich: Suffolk County Council, 1988), 22.
23 Mildred Campbell, *The English Yeoman* (London: Merlin Press, 1983 [1942]), 61.

Social changes also gave rise to new ideas of the family. The gentry and even the yeomanry were now identified not only by their traditional place of residence but by dynasty and lineage. With increasing social mobility it became more important to claim status through one's supposed ancestor.

In Norfolk, the Paston family had significant gentry status by the fifteenth century even though some claimed that they had emerged from lowly status a mere two centuries earlier. For such a family, there were new opportunities in holding office under the crown or even becoming lawyers even though the ownership of substantial land holdings still defined the class of gentry and gentlemen.[24]

By the early sixteenth century, both the gentry and the yeoman class were becoming predominant in Suffolk with many households in a number of parishes having holdings of over one hundred acres. There were many dominant yeomen particularly in East Suffolk. Some built up farms and livestock, developed industries such as tanning and employed labourers, others leased land from the local manor even while acting as a bailiff for the local lord.[25]

At the beginning of the seventeenth century, Robert Ryce a Suffolk-born member of the gentry, described Suffolk, where he had grown up. He celebrated a land of many rivers flowing to the sea, with 'aire . . . deemed to bee the purest' in England:

> This Country delighting in a coninuall evenes and plainness is void of any great hills, high mountains, or steep rocks, notwitstanding the which it is nott always so low, or flatt, butt that in every place, it is severed and devided with little hills easy for ascent and pleasant Ryvers watering the low valleys, with a most beautiful prospect which minstreth into the inhabitants a

---

24 Roger Virgoe, *Illustrated Letters of the Paston Family* (London: Macmillan, 1989).
25 Bailey, *Medieval Suffolk*, 248.

> full choice of healthfull and pleasant situations for their seemly houses.[26]

Ryce was particularly concerned with rank and status, recording the genealogy of Suffolk lords and gentry since the twelth century. But he also recognised other ranks including the 'poore' the 'husbandman' of small landholder, the 'townes-man', the 'gentleman' and

> our yeomanry, whose continuall vnder living, saving, and the immunities from the costly charge of these vnfaithfull times, do make them so to grow with the wealth of this world, that whilest many of the better sort, as having past their vttermost period do suffer an vtter declination, these only doe arise, and doe lay such strong, sure and deep foundations that thence in time are derived many noble and worthy families.[27]

It is this context of gentry and yeomanry that gave rise to the Sherington geneaology in East Anglia.

Sherington Genealogy

The Sheringtons have been living in the Suffolk village of Westleton from early to mid-sixteenth century. How long the family had been there is a matter of conjecture but it is highly likely that these Sheringtons had close associations with other Sheringtons across the nearby county border with Norfolk. The family name of Sherington can thus be said to have a genealogy based as much on locality as on family blood lines.

Westleton lies on the flat Suffolk coast protected from the sea by heathland. The soil in the area is sandy and the general coast-

26 Robert Ryce, *Suffolk in the XVIIth Century: The Breviary of Suffolk* (London: British Museum, 1902 [1618]), 23–25.
27 Ibid., 56–59.

line and parts of the hinterland in this part of Suffolk has long been known as the 'Sandlings'. The name of Westleton is Danish in origin, being one of the few settlements in Suffolk that carries this association. The name derives from an old Norse or Norwegian name, *Vestlidhi*, meaning a warrior who had travelled to the West (perhaps from Norway). Lying on the coast it may be assumed that the village was established with the 'Danish invasions' in the tenth century. Following the Norman invasion of 1066, a Domesday Book was compiled throughout England to establish a census of the population and the resources of the kingdom. At the time of the Domesday Book in 1086, Westleton had existed in a largely Saxon neighbourhood for a century and so the name had become 'Saxonised'. Thus, Westleton was originally spoken as *Vestlidhi's Tun* but was written in the Domesday Book as *Westelde's Tun*.[28]

The first recording of the Westleton population comes from the Domesday Book. Aki, a 'free man' had once held Westleton as a manor with thirteen villagers, and fourteen smallholders; previously there were also four slaves before the conquest but by 1086 there were none. The number of ploughs had been reduced from thirteen to five. There was also woodland and meadows for pigs, sheep and cattle. To a second manor belonged fourteen 'freemen' with a manor of over one hundred acres. A Gilbert Blunt held this manor from Robert Malet, the main Norman lord for Suffolk.[29]

By the time of the Domesday survey, Westleton, like many other villages in East Anglia, may have had two churches, one of which – St Peter's – still survives. There were also two manors known as Westleton and Westleton Grange, both owing allegiance to Robert Malet as tenant in chief, he being the son of William Malet, one of the great Norman magnates of Suffolk who

28 Alan Ivimey (ed.), *Westleton from the 1830s to the 1960s: Survey of a Suffolk Village* (Framlingham: Publication Committee of the Workers' Educational Association Westleton, 1968), 12.
29 Alex Rumble (ed.), *Domesday Book: Suffolk*, Part One (Chichester: Phillimore, 1986), 312 a, b.

had received 221 holdings in Suffolk. William Malet's main residence was the castle and borough of Eye (an old Anglo-Saxon market town in 'High' or central Suffolk close to the border with Norfolk), the estate being known as 'The Honour of Eye'. When Robert Malet plotted against the King in 1110, he was banished and the castle was taken into royal custody.[30]

Westleton Grange was soon transferred to the nearby Cistercian Abbey at Sibton founded in 1150 by monks from Yorkshire in close proximity to the village of Westleton. The 'advowson' or right of recommending a member of clergy for a vacant benefice was given to the abbey in respect of the church at Westleton in 1272 and appropriated in 1332. The abbey soon became the major landlord for surrounding villages and beyond. By the fifteenth century, the abbey held lands or rents in ten parishes in Norfolk and twenty-five parishes in Suffolk.[31] In the early sixteenth century, just prior to the dissolution of the monasteries by Henry VIII, Sibton Abbey possessed a number of enclosed farms with 1000 acres in total.[32]

As with other parts of Suffolk, the number of manors attached to Westleton increased from the eleventh century under the process known as 'subinfeudation' with the virtual break-up of the larger manors. This brought difficulties by the early fourteenth century. Disputes arose as to which lords had rights to hold manorial courts. By the fourteenth century, it seems that there were a total of eight manors that had been variously associated with the Westleton parish. Apart from Westleton Manor and Westleton Grange, there was Westleton Cleves and Minsmere, Lembaldes, Claydon's, Valen's and Rysing's.[33] By 1463 there were

30 Dymond and Northeast, *A History of Suffolk*, 35–36.
31 William Page (ed.), *The Victorian County History of the Counties of England: County of Suffolk*, vol. 2 (London: Archibald Constable, 1907), 89–90; A.H. Denney (ed.) *The Sibton Abbey Estates: Select Documents, 1325–1509* (Suffolk: Suffolk Records Society, 1960).
32 Joan Thirsk (ed.), *The Agrarian History of England and Wales*, vol. IV, *1500–1640* (Cambridge: Cambridge University Press, 1967), 310.

no less than fifteen lordships holding land in the parish. But there were also many manor houses going to waste.[34]

There were a number of influential owners associated with these Westleton manors. These included John Hopton, Yorkshire born in the fifteenth century, but inheriting estates in Norfolk, Suffolk as well as Nottinghamshire, Leicestershire and Derbyshire. In Westleton alone he held the Westleton Manor itself which now included the two manors of Valens as well as the manors of Lembaldes, Claydons and Rysings.[35] More generally his estates covered parts of the Blything Hundred which included Westleton and the nearby villages of Yoxford and Walberswick as well as the larger village of Blythburgh itself. Hopton was no absentee landlord, he lived in the area and was involved in developing his various demesne, although his lands at Westleton were leased for a period to the Abbey of Sibton.[36]

This form of diversified lordship with many manors and loose manorial controls was common throughout East Suffolk but had a particular impact at Westleton. The 'tenement' remained the common form of holding in medieval Suffolk involving traditional obligations to the local lord. But tenements became increasingly irregular in size and holding, passing from one owner to another. Even by the thirteenth century there was a market in land transfers. In the wake of the Norman invasion most land tenements had been associated with an individual but they served increasingly as a form of land title rather than an indication of current ownership and obligations. Thus twenty-two of the forty-nine persons listed as holders of land at Westleton in 1327 still remained on the 'title' of land at the end of the fifteenth century.[37]

---

33 P.M. Warner, 'Blything Hundred', PhD, University of Leicester, 1982, 214.

34 Ibid.

35 C. Richmond, *John Hopton: A Sixteenth Century Suffolk Gentleman* (Cambridge: Cambridge University Press, 1981), 25, 56–57.

36 Ibid., 57.

The effect of the Black Death had a major impact on not only population but the consolidation of land in East Suffolk. Early patterns of settlement had led to new hamlets and farms on the edges of the commons and 'greenfields'. Now 'isolated hamlets became isolated farms, and where a church may once have had two or three nearby, now it has none'.[38] By the mid-fifteenth century, the overall nature of tenements in Westleton had fallen into confusion. The records in 1463 indicated at least 164 tenements in Westleton, but not all had personal names attached to them and some were probably tenements in name only. There were also many 'waste cottages' listed but possibly because many tenements outside the parish also held land in Westleton. The overall structure of tenancy was becoming chaotic, the result of years of unrecorded sub-division, 'engrossing' and desertion.[39] The tiny acreage of one small tenement was spread over nine separate pieces over half the parish, with such holdings lying in three different manors until merged and gathered together.[40] Such conditions gave rise to the prospect of consolidation under a larger landholder. The dissolution of the monasteries then further stimulated the land market. The Abbey of Sibton lost its privileges and lands when they were transferred to the Duke of Norfolk under Act of Parliament in 1539.[41]

It is from the sixteenth century that the history of families and genealogy in England becomes easier to understand because of the actions of the Crown. First, from the reign of Edward VI the priest of each local parish was required to maintain a register of marriages, baptisms and deaths. Second, the 'Heraldic Visitations' which took place from 1530 to 1688 were designed

---

37 Peter Warner, *Greens, Commons and Clayland Colonization: The Origins and Development of Green-Side Settlement in East Suffolk* (Leicester: Leicester University Press, 1987), 34–35.
38 Ibid., 38.
39 Warner, 'Blything Hundred', 237
40 Ibid., 241.
41 Page, *The Victorian County History of the Counties of England*, 90.

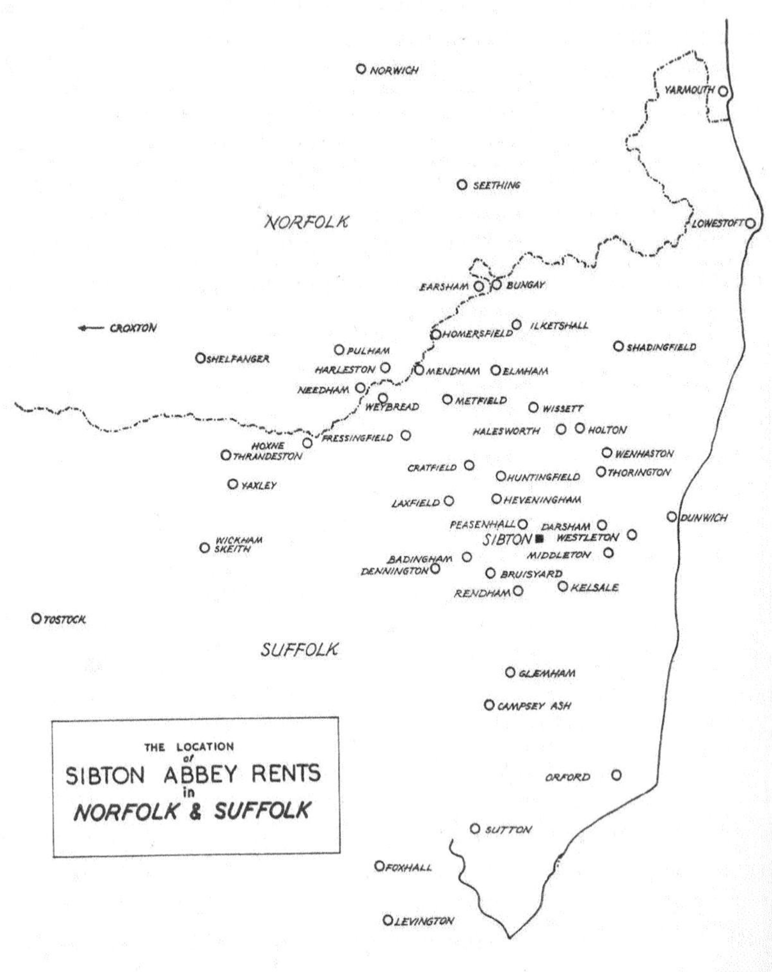

Sibton Abbey Rents in Norfolk and Suffolk. Westleton is just to the right of Sibton. Map available from A.H. Denney (ed.), *The Sibton Abbey Estates: Select Documents 1325–1509*, vol. 2 (Suffolk Records Society, 1960). For more information visit www.suffolkrecordssociety.com.

to regulate and register family coats of arms of the nobility and gentry and of boroughs and to record pedigrees. This was intended to sanction uses and prevent abuses of family coats of arms that had arisen in the fourteenth century. As a result, for a century and a half the monarchy licenced officers to visit various parts of the kingdom to gather information. The local sheriff was compelled to collect information from those displaying coats of arms. Coats of arms which were accepted were then registered in the College of Arms and recorded in volumes. While the College of Arms remains the official body for the register of Heraldry the Harleian Society was founded in 1869 to publish the manuscript visitations of the counties of England and Wales and other unpublished manuscripts such as those on family pedigree. Since its inception the Harleian Society has published more than ninety volumes of parish registers, fifty-four volumes of heraldic visitations and seventy volumes from other sources. Some of these are now online. This and other published research, along with our own detailed research into manorial records and wills has provided some indication of the history of the Sherington family in the fifteenth and particularly the sixteenth century.

There were also the impacts of nineteenth-century genealogical research. In the 1870s the Cambridge graduate, barrister and genealogist George William Marshall published *The Genealogist's Guide*, an extensive alphabetical listing by surname of the 'pedigrees' of numerous English families, defined by any 'printed descent' of three generations in the male line. The guide drew upon a variety of sources including listings of families in parish registers.[42] The family name of Sherington was listed in the guide as well as in several other sources including *The East Anglian*,

42 George Marshall, *The Genealogists Guide* (London: Bell and Sons, 1879). Republished in 1885, 1893 and 1903 and reprinted from 1967, this remains a standard work in English genealogy. See also Thomas Woodcock, 'Marshall, George William (1839–1905)', Oxford Dictionary of National Biography. [Online] Available: www.oxforddnb.com/view/article/34894. Accessed 24 December 2013.

a publication from the mid-nineteenth century which provided notes on Suffolk and family genealogies. *The East Anglian* arose out of the foundation of the Suffolk Institute of Archaeology, founded in 1848 and still in existence today. As initial secretary of the institute the antiquarian and bookseller and printer Samuel Tymms published a number of studies on wills as well as on the town of Bury St Edmunds in West Suffolk before editing and publishing *The East Anglian* from 1858. Tymms drew on local sources but also made certain conclusions which were not always substantiated. Thus volume three of the first four volumes of *The East Anglian* listed the 'Family of Sherington' in Westleton based on the parish registers from 1545 to 1767. It was also implied that the Sherington family originated from Cranworth in Norfolk.[43] How this possible Norfolk connection arose requires some discussion.

In the thirteenth century, during the reign of Henry III, Gregory De Sharenton owned land in the village of Sharington, Norfolk.[44] The family 'pedigree' of the Sharingtons (soon to be known as Sheringtons) was later established in the *Visitation of the County of Wiltshire*, 1565 and of *Worcestershire*, 1569 verifying a line of descent dating back to at least the fourteenth century. Ralph Sherington in the fourteenth century was a great-grandson of a John Sherington of Cranworth. Ralph had married the daughter of William de la Vale in Northumberland suggesting a connection with the North of England. The more formal and recognised beginning of the Sherington line of descent was in the fifteenth century through Henry Sherington who married Eliza-

---

43 'Family Sherington: Westleton Co. Suffolk' in Samuel Tymms (ed.), *The East Anglian*, vol. III (Lowestoft: S. Tymms; London: S. Whittaker, c.1858–69), 340–42. See also Robert Halliday, 'Tymms, Samuel (1808–1871)', Oxford Dictionary of National Biography. [Online] Available: www.oxforddnb.com/view/article/27946. Accessed 13 January 2014.

44 Francis Blomefield and Charles Parkin, *An Essay Towards the Topographical History of the County of Norfolk*, vol. X (London: William Miller, 1809), 198–201.

beth de Swathing of Cranworth (she having inherited Swathing manor from her father).[45] As the early-nineteenth-century genealogist Blomefield wrote, in words reflecting the relation between family, manor and church where one could still pray for the souls of the departed:

> Henry Sherington, Esq, who was steward to the bishop of Ely, for his hundred of Mitford, was lord of Swathing's in the 12 of Henry VI, and presented to this Church in 1435, and 1439; and Elizabeth his widow in 1452, and his son and heir Thomas in 1477, and 1487, who died about the 12 of Henry VII, and was succeeded by his son Thomas, Esq who presented in 1522.[46]

Grandson of Henry Sherington, Thomas Sherington married Katherine, daughter of Sir William Pyrton of Little Bentley Essex and his sole heir. They had five sons, William, Thomas, Henry, John and Anthony, and at least five daughters Elizabeth, Ann, Ursula, Olive and Cescille.[47]

As in the case of the Pastons in Norfolk, the emphasis on family names and family dynasty in the fifteenth- and sixteenth-centuries was often associated with regional and even national prominence of certain families who were part of the 'gentry' just below the aristocracy in the social structure of fifteenth and sixteenth century England. There were also the emerging 'burghers' of the urban centres which had long exercised their 'liberties' from local lords. In the North of England in the sixteenth cen-

---

45 Walter C. Metcalfe (ed.), *The Visitation of the County of Wiltshire, 1565* (London: Harleian Society, 1897), 241; William P. Phillimore (ed.), *The Visitation of the County of Worcestershire, 1569* (London: Harleian Society, 1889), 134–36.

46 Blomefield and Parkin, *An Essay Towards the Topographical History of the County of Norfolk*, 198–201. According to the College of Arms, Henry Sherington had four sons named as Reingold, Thomas, John, William: Reingold died without issue and Thomas inherited the manor. P. Gwynn Jones to Bruce Sherington, 2 October 1989.

47 P. Gwynn Jones to Bruce Sherington, 2 October 1989.

tury, members of a 'Sherrington' family were leading burghers and philanthropists associated with civic roles. In the early sixteenth century Geoffrey Sherrington, and Lawrence and James Sherrington were Mayors of Wigan. Francis Sherrington, 'a pious and philanthropic landlord and Mayor', founded Wigan Grammar School in 1894.[48] His brothers, William and Gilbert Sherrington, and other members of this Wigan Sherrington family were associated with either commerce or the law courts in London during the sixteenth century.[49] But there were also others by the name of Sherrington who were lawyers at the Inns of Court in London and who may have been cousins of the Wigan Sherringtons and even family associates of the Cranworth Sheringtons. According to the College of Arms, a grant of armorial bearings was made to William Sherrington of Grays Inn London in 1583.[50] This Sir William Sherrington was attested by an epitaph on a seventeenth-century church (destroyed in 1666) and with direct reference to Sheringtons of Cranworth in Norfolk:

> Sir William Sherrington, of Sherrington Hall and Cranworth, Kt of the selfsame line of that truly noble family of Sherringtons in Lancashire, from whence that heroical Collonel William Sherington [sic.], an eminent and successful commander in the Venetian service and also his very near and worthy kinsman William Sherrington, the Turkie merchant (with others of that removed race) are originally descended.[51]

---

48 Gordon Crewe Chambres, *History of Wigan Free Grammar School, 1596–1869* (Wigan: Thomas Wall, 1933), 61.
49 Gordon Crewe Chambres, *History of Wigan Free Grammar School, 1596–1869*, revised edition (Wigan: Thomas Wall, 1937), 98–103.
50 Gwynn Jones to Bruce Sherington, 2 October 1989.
51 Chambres, *History of Wigan Free Grammar School* (1937),104–05. Chambres, however, denies that there is any link between Sir William Sherington [sic.] and the Wigan Sherringtons when there obviously was.

By then, there had been more national prominence given to the deeds of another Sherington who may be directly related to the Sheringtons who appeared in the parish registers of Westleton in the sixteenth century. First son of Thomas and Katherine, William Sharington or Sherington of Cranworth Norfolk was born about 1495. It would seem that he had an early interest in art and architecture, having travelled to Italy. He soon had a patron in Sir Thomas Seymour who was attached to the court of Henry VIII. Having himself entered the service of the court of Henry VIII, Sherington of Cranworth Norfolk was knighted on the coronation of Edward VI. Having already acquired extensive property, in 1548 he became vice-treasurer of the mint at Bristol. He used his position at the mint to commit frauds. To prevent detection he entered into the plots of the Earl of Seymour against the Crown. Arrested and thrown into the Tower of London, he confessed to the frauds and connivance in Seymour's plots but was later pardoned and given new administrative posts. He recovered his property and was elected to Parliament. He died in 1553 with a reputation of being an 'administrator and embezzler'. A Hans Holbein sketch of Sherington is in the Royal Collection at Windsor Castle.[52]

Sir William Sherington was also a man of the Renaissance with interests in art and architecture. His most lasting legacy was the acquisition of the dissolved Lacock Abbey, Wiltshire in 1540, a site not far from Bristol mint where he acquired his wealth in illegal ways. The Countess of Salisbury had founded the abbey in the thirteenth century with support from Henry II who granted an enclosure of lands to support the nuns in the abbey. A thriving wool industry developed in the medieval village of Lacock, still standing nearby to the abbey. Sir William Sherington was able to benefit from Henry VIII's dissolution of religious houses to acquire the property. Influenced by the Renaissance and Italian art

52 C.E. Challis, 'Sharington, Sir William (c.1495–1553)' in *Oxford Dictionary of National Biography* (Oxford: Oxford University Press, 2004).

he then converted the abbey into a residential house while retaining much of the medieval building.[53]

While Sir William Sherington thus preserved the abbey for posterity it would not pass down to his own descendants for while he married three times he had no children. After Sir William died in 1553 the abbey passed to his brother Henry. Elizabeth I supposedly then knighted Henry Sherington after he invited her to a meal at the abbey. Henry married Anne, daughter of Robert Paget. They had no sons but three daughters, Ursula, Grace and Olive. The youngest, Olive, eventually inherited the estate and married into the Talbot family of Worcestershire at first retaining the name of Sharington-Talbot through her descendants. The Talbot family continued to reside continuously at Lacock Abbey until the 1940s. In the nineteenth century William Talbot Fox, one of the pioneers of photography, used the abbey as a studio to pattern the development of negatives. In the twenty-first century Lacock Abbey is one of the most significant surviving Abbeys in England, constituting part of the heritage of the National Trust.

The purchase of Lacock Abbey relocated the fortunes and focus of most of the the Sherington family from Norfolk to Wiltshire. After purchasing Lacock Abbey Sir William Sherington had then conveyed the family manor of Swathing in Norfolk to Sir Richard Southwell who had assumed the title of lord of the manor by 1546.[54] Other members of the Sherington family had also moved on from Norfolk. John Sherington, the younger brother of both Sir William and Sir Henry, by then resided in Medborne Wiltshire, and had three sons, Edward, Oliver, and one other male whose name is not known.[55]

53 National Trust, *Lacock Abbey* (London: National Trust, 1996).

54 Blomefield and Parkin, *An Essay Towards the Topographical History of the County of Norfolk*, 201.

55 Letter, Jones to Bruce Sherington, 2 October 1989.

While Sir William Sherington, and at least two of his brothers, had re-located to Wiltshire, parts of the older generation of Norfolk Sheringtons had moved to Suffolk. Two of the sisters of Sir William and Sir Henry: Cecilia Sherington married Robert Southwell (Serjeant at Law) and was buried at Barham Suffolk; and Anne Sherington married Edmund Playters of Suffolk. Both the Southwells and Playters were listed as part of the county 'knights' in 1561.[56] The Playters in particular were one of the most significant gentry families in Suffolk from the fourteenth century to the eighteenth century. With a manor estate at Soterley in north-east Suffolk the Playters had been 'resident gentry' in the area since the Middle Ages. They also had long had associations with the gentry of Norfolk, including the Pastons.[57] A marriage alliance between the Playters and the Sheringtons was obviously a significant reflection of social status and position.

What then of the origins of the Sheringtons in Westleton where their names appear in the parish registers from the early sixteenth century? There were visitations to Suffolk in 1561, 1577 and 1612. On this basis, lists of family 'pedigrees' were compiled based principally on lineage and proven descent over a number of generations. Most families were identified in respect to their estates and land holdings as well as the local manor or village. The only record of a 'family pedigree' based on Westleton was the Brockett family who had originated from Hertfordshire, although the lineage of John Hopton, who held extensive manorial holdings at Westleton, was noted in respect to the village of Westwood.[58]

---

56 Walter C. Metcalfe (ed.), *The Visitations of Suffolk Made by Hervey Clarenceux, 1561, Cooke, Clarenceux, 1577, and Raven, Richmond Herald, 1612, with Notes and an Appendix of Additional Suffolk Pedigrees* (Exeter: William Pollard, 1882).

57 Dymond and Northeast, *A History of Suffolk*, 81; Roger Virgoe, *Illustrated Letters of the Paston Family*, 110, 114, 117. By the reign of James I, Thomas Playters was High Sheriff for Suffolk, being able to ride from Beccles to Dunwich, a trip of fifteen miles, all on his own land. Alan Jobson, *Suffolk Villages* (London: Robert Hale, 1971), 38.

In 1940, the genealogist Arthur Campling, published *East Anglian Pedigrees* under the auspices of the Norfolk Records Society which had been formed in 1930 to publish and make accessible records and documents relating to the history of Norfolk (the book was published almost simultaneously in 1940 by the Harleian Society). This publication was a 'selection' of Camplings' – almost half a century of genealogical research, concentrating on the 'pedigrees' of families in East Anglia not previously published (such as in the Visitations). Thus the 'greater number of pedigrees are those of families remaining in the yeoman class or emerging to the status of gentry and outside the purview of most county historians'.[59]

Drawing on parish registers and associated documents Campling published the origins and family trees of 170 East Anglian families. Some entries, including that for his own family, went back to the thirteenth century but most began in the sixteenth century. Of the 170 entries, the vast majority were of Norfolk families, with only thirty-seven being for those from Suffolk. Included was the following heading for the family of Sherington:

> Sherington of Westleton County, Suffolk
> William Cudon alias Sherinton of Westleton 1510[60]

It is not entirely clear how Campling had reached this conclusion for apparently he left no notes on his research. But the entry would suggest that William Cudon, who also went by the name of Sherinton, was the founder of the Sherington family at Westleton from 1510. Equally, in an age where there were often still two surnames attributed to an individual this may imply some asso-

58 Metcalfe, 1882.
59 Arthur Campling (ed.) *East Anglian Pedigrees* (Norfolk: Norfolk Record Society, 1940), xxiii. The Harleian Society published this as volume 91 of its publications in 1939; a second related, but slighter volume 97 appeared in 1945 after Campling had died.
60 Ibid., 200.

ciation between the Sheringtons and Cudon family, whereby a William Cudon had also assumed the family name of Sherington. To understand this possibility it is necessary first to outline the place of the Cudon family along the coast of Suffolk.

The Cudon or Codon family had been long associated with Dunwich the sea port which lay on the coast as Westleton's next door neighbour. Dunwich probably began as an Anglo-Saxon sea port but it soon had one of the first schools in England and had early church associations. The first Christian bishop in East Anglia, St Felix, had supposedly held his seat at *Domnoc* usually interpreted to mean Dunwich, or 'hill by the winding river' implying that the settlement was once inland on a hill by the river, but the erosion of the coastline brought it closer to the sea.[61] By the time of the Norman Conquest Dunwich had become a prized possession. The Domesday Book of 1086 indicated a town of some size. There was a small manor attached of only two small landholders with Robert Malet the lord of the manor but also forty 'Frenchmen' with forty acres of land paying 'customary due' to the lord and 236 'burgesses' or free men in the town plus 178 'poor men'.[62]

Dunwich soon was seen as a major centre on the Suffolk coast:

> In its heyday, about the time of King John, Dunwich was a gated town on a hill about forty feet above the sea. Within its gates stood eight, possibly nine, parish churches and a number of religious houses. In its market places, markets were held every day of the week.[63]

---

61 Warner, *The Origins of Suffolk*, 127–33; Dymond and Northeast, *A History of Suffolk*, 30. See also Norman Gay, *Glorious Dunwich: Its Story Throughout the Ages* (Suffolk: Suffolk Press, 1946).

62 Rumble, *Domesday Book: Suffolk*, 311 b, 312 a.

63 Scarfe, *The Suffolk Landscape*, 207.

By the fourteenth century, the sea had begun to advance on Dunwich. On just one day in 1327, waves 'chocked the ancient harbour with shingle and forced the river's mouth away to the north, towards the territory of (the nearby village) Blythburgh'.[64] Dunwich had a tense relation with its neighbours, such as Blythburgh and Westleton, and tried to insist on its right to maintain access to and from the sea. Eventually both the seas and trade began to turn against Dunwich. In the fifteenth century, Iceland and the North Sea had been profitable fields of fishing and trade for many of the coastal towns of Suffolk. The foreign and coastal trade produced boat building and related industries leading to high concentrations of taxpayers along the Suffolk coast.[65] But following the Reformation there was an increasing demand for fish with increasing competition and piracy. And then the advancing sea began to erode the coast. By the end of the sixteenth century not only was Dunwich blocked off from the sea but so were other nearby ports such as Orford and Walberswick.[66] By the end of the seventeenth century Dunwich was 'impoverished' and almost three quarters of the town's population was exempt from paying tax. As with other coastal ports houses had been abandoned.[67]

Despite its precarious position, Dunwich was one of only six towns in Suffolk with borough status and 'liberties' granted by the crown. Medieval towns have been described as 'free islands in feudal seas'. Burgesses were the 'freemen' within boroughs with the 'burghal elite' often holding both urban and rural land holdings. Amongst Dunwich's most important burgers from the eleventh to fourteenth centuries were the Codons.[68] By the fourteenth century Peter Codon was one of the wealthiest burgers in

---

64 Ibid., 208.

65 Todd & Dymond, 'Population Densities, 1327 and 1524', 64.

66 Dymond and Northeast, *A History of Suffolk*, 68.

67 Nesta Evans, 'People and Poor in 1674' in David Dymond and Edward Martin (eds), *An Historical Atlas of Suffolk* (Ipswich: Suffolk County Council, 1988), 78.

Dunwich, a member of the council assisting the 'bailiff' (mayor), and serving as one of Dunwich's two members elected to the Parliament held in 1410. The Codons soon became involved in the legal dispute between Dunwich and the neighbouring village of Walberswick over Dunwich's traditional rights to levy tolls on coastal trade and rights of access to the sea. The local lord, Roger Swillington, took the side of Walberswick, which triumphed in the legal cause. A further embarrassment was that the Codons held a small manor in Westleton where Swillington was chief lord.[69]

What may have partly affected the alliegances of the Cudons was the changing status of Dunwich. Neither Henry VII nor Henry VIII held the town in favour. Henry VIII dissolved all the monasteries associated with Dunwich. There were also natural disasters. By the mid-sixteenth century storms were again devastating the town.[70] By the mid-fifteenth century, the Codons had already become substantial tenants in Westleton, holding a number of other rural manors in Suffolk, and retaining their holdings into the sixteenth century while maintaining their positions in Dunwich including representing the borough of Dunwich in the House of Commons.[71] The Suffolk visitation of 1561 indicated that the Cudon pedigree was located also in the village of Weston in the north-east part of the county and thus not far from Westleton. By the 1616 Visitation there were also Cuddons at nearby Shaddingfield in north-east Suffolk.[72] Of most significance, the Cudons had married into the Playter family just as the

---

68 R. Parker, *Men of Dunwich: The Story of a Vanished Town* (New York: Holt, Rhinehart & Winston, 1979), 159, 170, 239, 249.
69 Mark Bailey, *The Bailiffs' Book of Dunwich,1404–1430*, Suffolk Records Society publication XXXIV (Woodbridge: The Boydell Press, 1992), 4–15. The minute book contains numerous reference to the Codons indicating their overall position in terms of wealth and land holdings.
70 Gay, *Glorious Dunwich*, 26.
71 Bailey, *Medieval Suffolk*, 136; Richmond, *John Hopton*, 56.
72 Metcalfe, *The Visitations of Suffolk*, 23, 131.

Sheringtons from Norfolk had formed a marriage alliance with the Playters.

Such marriage and family dynasty alliances may explain why a Cudon might have assumed the name of 'Sherington'. The *East Anglian Pedigrees* entry for the Sherington family also assumes this occurred from 1510. But the subsequent family tree in *East Anglian Pedigrees* indicates that genealogical line is then traced through 'Thomas Sherington of Westleton yeoman'.[73] This reference to Thomas Sherington of Westleton has raised other some possibilities for he was obviously of the same generation as Sir William Sherington of Norfolk, and then Lacock Abbey, who had a brother known as Thomas. So rather than being a direct descendent of William Cudon, was this Thomas Sherington of Westleton actually the brother of Sir William Sherington?

Initially this was considered a strong possibility. And to strengthen this view there was a Thomas Sherington who appeared in the Norfolk Subsidy (for taxation purposes) of 1523–24 for the parish of Hingham near to the Sherington family residence at Cranworth in Norfolk. He was connected to the Jenner family who had also formed a marriage with the Playters. By the 1530s, a Thomas Sherington appeared in the manorial rolls for Westleton buying land in the 1530s.[74]

But there are certain qualifications which make this connection between Thomas Sherington of Westleton and Sir William Sherington less certain. According to the *Visitation of Wiltshire 1565* Sir William's brother Thomas, formally the next in line to Sir William, had no issue, and his younger brother Henry inherited Lacock Abbey, also implying that Thomas had predeceased Sir William.[75] To reinforce the fact that Thomas Sherington, brother of Sir William, had no children it has been pointed out that

---

73 Campling, *East Anglian Pedigrees*, 200.

74 Letter, Bruce Sherington to Joanna Martin, 11 November 1991.

75 William Harvey, *Visitation of Wiltshire, 1565* (London: Harliean Society, 1897), 241.

while Sir William Sherington did not leave a will there was an inquistion post mortem which did not mention any heirs that Thomas had (even though Thomas of Westleton died in 1552 a year before Sir William, and if he was Sir William's brother, perhaps there was no need to mention any heirs he had).[76] There is also the fact that Campling's research for *East Anglian Pedigrees* suggested that Thomas Sherington of Westleton was a yeoman and this might suggest he was not of the status of gentry equivalent to Sir William and his family.

As with the name of Cudon being associated with Sherington, the identity of Thomas Sherington of Westleton is in some senses a mystery now difficult to resolve due to the passage of time and problems of associating specific individuals with names. If Campling was right in the Cudon association to the Sheringtons at Westleton it may also be an indication of the merger of the lesser branches of two gentry families, rather than a direct line through either. But what is certain is that from the mid-sixteenth century the name and the family of Sherington was now more in Suffolk than Wiltshire or even Norfolk.

This may all show that in general overall family connections and blood lines between Norfolk and Suffolk were often very common, particularly on the coast of East Suffolk. Of particular significance were the role of Dukes of Norfolk and the extended Howard family. After the Norman Conquest much of the land holdings in Medieval Norfolk was in the hands of the crown or sometimes absentee nobles.[77] In the fourteenth century the Duke of Norfolk and the Earl of Suffolk were contestants for influence in East Anglia. But during the reign of Henry VIII, Thomas, third Duke of Norfolk supplanted the Earl of Suffolk and came to exercise great influence at the royal court as Earl Marshall and Treasurer of England. Two of Henry's six wives, Anne Boelyn and Catherine Howard, both executed, were members of the ex-

76 Notes of Joanna Martin.
77 Martins, *A History of Norfolk*, 1997, 31–50.

tended Howard family. With already large holdings in Norfolk and along the coast of East Suffolk, the third duke enriched himself further through the dissolution of the monasteries, acquiring land of various religious houses, including Sibton Abbey near Westleton.[78]

In 1532 three inhabitants of Westleton even turned to the Duke of Norfolk seeking help for relief of a debt of sixty pounds to the King, the result of them having forfeited bonds for their vicar and a neighbour. Although the duke had no property in Westleton, their instinct was to turn to him for help, with one of his manors being just twenty miles north. Through a series of blunders by the Westleton supplicants the duke could eventually do little for these 'Westleton unfortunates' but access had been provided from their 'coastal heathland' village into the household of the King.[79]

Suffolk thus remained tied to Norfolk in many ways. But we can also conclude that from the sixteenth century a particular line of the Sherington family would become part of the life of Westleton on the Suffolk coast. The link to other Sheringtons, such as Sir William Sherington is not clear, but what is certain is that the Sheringtons in Westleton from the mid-sixteenth century held substantial land holdings for farming.

Westleton Yeomen

From the early sixteenth century to the late eighteenth century it is clear that Sheringtons were yeomen in the village of Westleton in East Suffolk. Thomas Sherington – also apparently known as Cudon – would create the beginnings of a family dynasty line in Westleton with his wife Margery. Probably born in about

---

78 John Martin Robinson, *The Dukes of Norfolk: A Quincentennial History* (Oxford: Oxford University Press, 1982), 38.

79 Diarmaid MacCulloch, *Suffolk and the Tudors: Politics and Religion in an English County, 1500–1600* (Oxford: Clarendon Press, 1986), 226–27.

1500, possibly a 'cousin' of Sir William Sherington, or with some associations to the village of Sherington in Norfolk, he was undoubtedly a yeoman or farmer with substantial land, taking advantage of new economic and social possibilities.

By the 1530s the growth of population was forcing up the price of land and food throughout England. Market towns which had developed in the medieval period generally expanded along with other private buyers. The village and lands of Westleton were part of that stretch of loams and sands agricultural land extending in a broad arc from south-west Suffolk up into Norfolk and then down the coast of Suffolk. Here mixed sheep–corn husbandry prevailed with the sheep providing the fertilizer for the corn as well as being fed for market. And Suffolk farmers soon became known for innovations, growing hops and hemp, and developing agricultural implements such as ploughs and harrows.[80]

When Thomas Sherington died in 1550, he had lands in the manor of Westleton of approximately twenty acres in total. These included a 'customary tenement' of four acres called 'Costyns in Woodstrete'. There was also a piece of 'customary land' of ten acres the known as the 'Lower Baldmans', 'Upper Baldmans' and 'Baldmans Fields'; one piece of 'customary land' of the 'tenement Palmers'; three acres of land formerly of a John Brundysche and a piece of customary land of two acres.[81] The terminology would indicate the medieval past of land tenure now undergoing change through consolidated individual holdings. The actual names were thus traditional or probably associated with those long dead.

Thomas' second-born son William Sherington and his wife Joane had eleven children born between 1569 and 1587 with seven known to have survived childhood. When William died in 1595 he left a will initially leaving to his wife 'all my houses and

80 Thirsk, *The Agrarian History of England and Wales*, 41–44.
81 Westleton Court Rolls, HA30:50/22/11.1 (3) Suffolk Records Office Ipswich and Bruce Sherington, research notes based on Wills and later ordnance surveys of Westleton and surrounding fields.

lands lyinge or being in Westleton' which would then pass after two years to his son Thomas. All his money was to be divided amongst his five younger children. His 'wiffe was to have half my shepe' with the other half going to all the children. His son 'Williame' would receive a 'yereling hefker' while 'silver spoons' and 'puetter platters' also formed part of the estate to be distributed to members of the family. Finally there was special provision for his wife to be provided by his eldest son and principal heir Thomas. After two years had elapsed, his wife would continue to have the 'parlour chamber' of the main residence and Thomas would pay his mother 'forty shelinges' a year provided that she made no further claim on the lands in his estate. And finally Thomas was to receive 'my shod cartte' as a clear reflection of being a working farmer.[82]

By the late sixteenth century the Sheringtons were well established in Westleton. The Westleton parish registers indicate a growing extended Sherington family line. By the mid-seventeenth century, the Sherington dynasty in Suffolk also took in coastal towns of Lowestoft and Yarmouth. Indeed Campling's Sherington family tree focuses more on the Yarmouth area, leaving the need to understand those who remained in Westleton from wills as well as the surviving parish registers.[83]

John Sherington, who was the oldest son of the initial Thomas Sherington in Westleton, was declared highest village taxpayer in 1568 holding seven pounds in lands.[84] He held extensive known holdings of almost thirty acres spread across a number of manors in Westleton. Significantly, this included land formerly held by a Peter Cooden (Cuddon) and other land of Thomas Brundishe. He held a freehold 'large arable close' in the Bellaymes formerly held by Brundishe, (so apparently consolidating Sher-

---

82 IC/AA1/33/224 and IC/AA2/35/455 Suffolk Record Office, Ipswich.

83 Campling, *East Anglian Pedigrees*, 200–02.

84 *Suffolk in 1568: Being the Return for a Subsidy Granted in 1566*, Suffolk Green Books, vol. XII, (Bury St Edmunds: Paula Matthew, 1909), 53.

ington holdings in this field) as well as fifteen acres of 'customary hold' of the manors of Cleves and Risings and two acres of customary land of the manor of Westleton. Finally,

> John Sherington holds a freehold messuage of the manor of Cleves, formerly held by Thomas Brundishe, with a house, gardens &c., lying on the east of the said large enclosure and abutting on the said common way on the north of the manor of Westleton on the south.[85]

Acquistions and property were now seen not just in farming land. The new wealth of the Elizabeth Age of the sixteenth century had led to the establishment of grand country homes of the gentry with formal living, entertaining rooms and bedrooms. The life of yeomen was not so grand but still comfortable. Many homes of farmers were in the local village, where the tasks of farming often intruded into the home. The 'backhouse' was often attached to the main house as a service room for cooking, brewing, baking, and similar purposes. The homes of wealthier yeomen sometimes had several service rooms. One Suffolk 'husbandman' had a house with eight rooms, a stable and a barn. Two ground floor chambers were bedrooms, and at the other end of the house was a buttery, a kitchen and backhouse. A chamber over the hall and a solar over the buttery were to be used for storage.[86]

When Thomas Sherington, grandson of the original Thomas Sherington of Westleton, composed his will in 1638 he allowed for the inheritance of both land and domestic furniture. He had now acquired further land known as the 'Lamb Pits' (possibly pits of lime for sheep carcasses).[87] But the opening paragraphs of

---

85 Survey of Claydon's and other manors in Westleton, 1569–70, Suffolk Records Office, Ipswich.
86 M.W. Barley, 'Rural Housing in England' in Thirsk (ed.), *The Agrarian History of England and Wales*, vol. IV, 720–21.
87 Bruce Sherington, research notes.

his last will and testament mentioned his wife, Temperance, to whom he gave:

> one stand-bedsteade, with the feather bed, coverlinges, boulsters, pillows, cuteynes, and all other thinges, thereunto belonging as yt standeth in my parlour, And besides six pewter platters, and what and how much brasse and lyneth she pleaseth to take out of all my brass and lynne.

Thomas, his eldest son, inherited 'all my lands and Tenemente both ffree and coppye which I had by inheritance from my father' on condition that Thomas then provided five pounds to four of his siblings William, Robert, John and Elizabeth. Should Thomas fail to carry this out, then these four children would receive 'one pictle of my coppye hold land lyinge in Westleton commonlye called & known by the name of long pictle'. Thomas was also to receive 'one pictle of more of freehold land lyinge in Westleton at Lampetts which I bought of one Mr Green' on condition that Thomas provide to his other sister 'ffrances', who was now married to John Crispe of Westleton, the sum of 'twentye shillings yearly'. Thomas was also to receive his father's 'cownter table standinge in my hall'.[88]

The standing of the Sheringtons in Westleton also needs to be seen in a wider context. From the sixteenth century, Suffolk was a highly literate society with more than ninety per cent of clergy and more than sixty per cent of the yeomen and craftsmen being able to read and write. By the mid-sixteenth century all the 'gentlemen' of Southern England were literate, perhaps a century before those in the North.[89] Literacy was closely associated with ideas of 'independence'. By the seventeenth century, much of Suffolk was composed of independent-minded and anti-Catholic middle-class Puritans who would oppose the efforts of King

88 IC/AA1/74/143 and IC/AA2/64/61 Ipswich Record Office.
89 MacCulloch, *Suffolk and the Tudors*, 316–17.

Charles I to impose royal authority. On religious and economic grounds some left Suffolk forever, emigrating to North America and becoming part of the Puritan plantations in the colony of Massachusetts. Amongst them was John Winthrop later founder of the College of Harvard.[90]

Westleton seemed to escape much of the political strife of the seventeenth century with the parliamentary revolt, execution of Charles I and the establishment of the republic. The vast majority of gentry families in Suffolk remained neutral during these troubles; on the coast near Westleton there was a slight preference of support for the royalist cause.[91] But as elsewhere in Suffolk, Westleton suffered the extremes of religious intolerance during this period. In 1641, the Puritan influenced English Parliament resolved that all 'superstitious' pictures and inscriptions in churches be removed and defaced. William Dowsing, a native of Suffolk, was given charge of such a task and in less than fifty days he and his troops swept through 150 Suffolk churches on a campaign of defacement and destruction of memorials, relics and reminders of the Catholic past. Included in these acts of vandals were the churches of Walberswick and Blythburgh, neighbouring villages to Westleon.[92] Westleton seems to have survived this outrage perhaps because its church, St Peter's, had little decoration on wall or window – a condition which still remains in the twenty-first century.

For the most part there was continuing prosperity in Suffolk until well into the eighteenth century. The Sherington family biographies in the Appendix suggest that the family was doing well throughout the sixteenth to the eighteenth century. Suffolk became known for experiment and specialisation, the first county

90 Dymond and Northeast, *A History of Suffolk*, 73.

91 Gordon Blackwood, 'The Gentry of Suffolk During the Civil War' in David Dymond and Edward Martin (eds), *An Historical Atlas of Suffolk* (Ipswich: Suffolk County Council, 1988), 84.

92 C.H. Evelyn White (ed.), *The Journal of William Dowsing* (Ipswich: Pawsey Hayes, 1885), 59–60.

to grow turnips. There were now quite distinct regions of agriculture. To the north-west of Bury St Edmunds was a landscape of virtually medieval fields focusing on crops and sheep. 'High Suffolk' in the centre of the county had mixed farming with dairying. Westleton was part of the 'Sandlings' on the coast, containing extensive marshlands which required draining.[93]

Much was achieved from the sixteenth to the eighteenth century. By the end of the eighteenth century, Suffolk was known as a county where there had been improvement in farming methods. When Arthur Young, the influential economist and agricultural scientist, and secretary of the Board of Agriculture, reported on Suffolk in 1813, he was particularly impressed by the farms in the 'Sandlings':

> This district I take to be one of the best cultivated in England; not exempt from faults and deficiencies, but having many features of unquestionably good management. It is also a most profitable one to farm in; and there are few districts in the county, if any, abounding with wealthier farmers, nor any that contain a greater proportion of occupying proprietors, possessing from one hundred to three and four hundred pounds a year.[94]

Arcadia Portrayed

By the end of the eighteenth century Suffolk was not just a prosperous county. In the wider public consciousness, through visual and literary representations, Suffolk prompted almost idlyic images of rural southern England. A number of the major artists and literary figures of eighteenth century England owed much of their inspiration and reputations to Suffolk. Born in Sudbury,

93 Dymond and Northeast, *A History of Suffolk*, 91–92.
94 Arthur Young, *General View of the County of Suffolk* (Newtown Abbott: David and Charles reprints, 1968 [reprint of 1813 edition]), 5.

Suffolk in 1699 Thomas Gainsborough became renowned for his portraits of English aristocracy and gentry but he also influenced a generation of Suffolk artists with his landscapes often containing 'rustic figures' in the English countryside.[95] Amongst these were John Constable born in East Bergholt (near the Suffolk border with Essex) in 1776 and the most famous of all English landscape artists in the late eighteenth and early nineteenth century. With his work on the Stour River (Dedham Valley) Constable strove to get a 'pure and unaffected representation' of what lay before him in the scenes of rural Suffolk. As he later remembered this place of his birth:

> its gentle declivities, its luxuriant meadow flats sprinkled with flocks and herds, its well cultivated uplands, its woods and rivers, with numerous scattered villages and churches, farms and picturesque cottages.[96]

Through Constable and later other landscape painters, Suffolk came to represent much that was seen as uniquely rural English arcadia.

Poets with a national audience and reputation also created images of rural life in eighteenth-century Suffolk. Robert Bloomfield was born in 1766 in the village of Honnington not far from Westlcton. Coming from humble circumstances Bloomfield attended the local 'dame's school' and then went to London to practise the trade of shoemaking. But he retained an affection for his days in the country later writing the poem 'The Farmer's Boy', an elegy on the cycle of the seasons in Suffolk. With patronage from dukes and even the Prince of Wales, the poem was later published in 1800 and in three years had sold 30 000 copies.

---

95 Chloe Bennett, *Suffolk Artists, 1750–1930: Paintings from the Ipswich Borough Museums & Galleries Collections* (Ipswich: Images Publication & Ipswich Borough Council, 1991).

96 Leslie Parris, *Constable Pictures from the Exhibition* (London: Tate Gallery, 1991), 11.

Bloomfield captured the imagination of an urban middle-class audience celebrating the English countryside. The opening verses suggest a Suffolk spring with joys more than comparable to other natural wonders such as found in the Alps on the Continent.

The Farmer's Boy
Spring.
O Come, blest Spirit! Whatsoe'er thou art,
Thou rushing warmth that hover'st round my heart,
Sweet inmate, hail! Thou source of sterling joy,
That poverty itself cannot destroy,
Be thou my Muse; and faithful still to me,
Retrace the paths of wild obscurity.
No deeds of arms my humble lines rehearse;
No Alpine wonders thunder through my verse,
The roaring cataract, the snow-topt hill,
Inspiring awe, till breath itself stands still:
Nature's sublimer scenes ne'er charm'd mine eyes,
Nor Science led me through the boundless skies;
From meaner objects far my raptures flow;
O point these raptures! Bid my bosom glow!
And lead my soul to ecstasies of praise
For all the blessings of my infant days!
Bear through me through regions where gay Fancy dwells;
But mould to Truth's fair form what Memory tells.[97]

Bloomfield's verse has sometimes been compared to the other eighteenth-century celebrated Suffolk poet George Crabbe who

---

97 William Wickett and Nicolas Duval, *The Farmer's Boy: the Story of a Suffolk Poet Robert Bloomfield, his Life and Poems, 1766–1823* (Lavenham: Terence Dalton, 1971), 70.

was born in Aldeburgh (on the coast but south of Dunwich) and who later made his reputation in London through associations with the politician Edmund Burke. Crabbe had hoped to be a surgeon but became a clergyman and soon a well-known poet. Both Bloomfield and Crabbe wrote poetry in iambic pentameter couplets. Bloomfield tended to celebrate the life he remembered as a young man. Crabbe continued to cast his eye over the nature of village and community life as an observer. His best known collection of poems, *The Borough*, published in 1810, contains description of a Suffolk sea port (obviously Aldeburgh) in a series of twenty-four letters on such topics as 'the church', 'the vicar', 'the curate', 'sects and professions in religion', 'the election', 'professions-law' 'professions-physic', 'trades' 'amusements' 'clubs and social meetings', 'inns', 'players', 'the almshouse and trustees', 'inhabitants of the alms-house', 'the hospital and governors', 'the poor and their dwellings', 'the poor of the borough', 'the parish clerk', 'prisons' and 'schools'. Amongst the characters Crabbe described was Peter Grimes, the fisherman which later formed the basis of the twentieth-century Benjamin Britten opera of the same name.[98]

Through his poetry Crabbe provides an understanding of the life of eighteenth-century Suffolk. He obviously understood the aspirations, fears and foibles of all social classes in the county. Such was the theme in his later 'Gentleman Farmer', published in a series of *Tales* as a supplement to *The Borough* and other works.

> Two are the species in this genus known:
> One, who is rich in his profession grown,
> Who yearly finds his ample stores increase,
> From fortune's favours and a favouring lease;

98 *The Life and Poetical Works of Rev George Crabbe By His Son* (London: John Murray, 1866), 175–279.

Who rides his hunter, who his house adorns;
Who drinks his wine, and his disbursement scorns;
Who freely lives, and loves to show he can –
This is the Farmer made the Gentleman.
The second species from the world is sent,
Tired with its strife, or with his wealth content;
In books and men beyond the former read,
To farming by a passion led,
Or by a fashion; curious in his land;
Now planning much, now changing what he plann'd;
Pleased by each trial, not by failures vex'd,
And ever certain to succeed the next;
Quick to resolve, and easy to persuade, –
This is the Gentleman, a Farmer made.[99]

Crabbe's verse suggests the changing social origins and even status of Suffolk yeomen farmers, some of whom aspired to be 'gentlemen' while gentlemen now wished to become farmers. By the late eighteenth century, the Suffolk countryside had become much the possession of the comfortable landowners. It was a county in which they at least could live and behold the beauty around them. It was also place to visit and admire. The publication of travel guides began with the spread of the coach routes. And much emphasis was placed on the apparent 'antiquity' of a place as well as 'lineage' of families. The clergyman Thomas Cromwell, a resident of London, was a Fellow of the Society of Antiquaries and a scholar who helped to compose guides to the English Counties. The two-volume *Excursions in the Country of Suffolk* published in 1816 with extensive illustrations and engrav-

99 Ibid., 286.

ings provided 'Historical and Topographical Delineation of Every along Town and Village' along with 'Descriptions of the Residences of the Nobility and Gentry', the 'Remains of Antiquity' and 'Every Other Object of Curiosity' for the traveller and tourist. Of Westleton there was but brief reference in Volume 2 to a parish which 'once contained a hamlet, which had a chapel belonging to it named Dingle' as well as the four manors of 'Westleton, Westleton Grange, which once belonged to the Abbey of Sibton, Westleton Cleves, and Minsmere, or Scott's Hall'.[100] There was much more fascination with the 'great antiquity' of nearby Dunwich, much of whose medieval past now lay under the sea while the town remnants clung to the side of a cliff:

> Dunwich, now esteemed a mean village, stands on a cliff of considerable height, commanding an extensive view of the German ocean, about four miles south of Southwold. The market is held here on Mondays. Here at present about 40 houses and 208 inhabitants; and an annual fair is held on St James's day and the 25th of July for toys etc.[101]

In the late eighteenth and early nineteenth century Westleton had only one family which could properly be described as 'gentry'. Although the village had been attached to eight manors in the medieval period there was now no large country mansion or park. The Woods family, however, had been associated with the village for centuries. There were many eighteenth-century memorials to the Woods in St Peter's Church. But even their influence was in decline. By the mid-nineteenth century there were 6000 acres for cultivation in the village and its fields of which two-thirds was owned by two absentee landlords living outside the parish. Of the remaining third, there were another nine different land-

---

100 Thomas Cromwell, *Excursions in the County of Suffolk*, vol. 2 (London: Longman Hurst, 1816), 123.
101 Ibid., 130.

lords owning forty acres each, leaving 235 acres divided between twenty-five different landowners, even some of these living outside the parish.[102]

Arcadia in Suffolk and in Westleton itself was in effect reserved principally for the few. And by the end of the eighteenth century many in the Sherington family were living only on the margins of rural prosperity.

Decline and Renewal

Changing patterns of ownership throughout parts of mid- to late-eighteenth-century Suffolk spelt the end of many smaller yeomen farmers and the rise of more substantial landowners assisted by the enclosure of the commons and woodlands that began as early as the sixteenth century and continued under Acts of Parliament in the eighteenth century. The growth of the population during the late eighteenth century also meant that opportunities for many farming families were declining. In the decades 1750–70 and then again in 1780–90 the number of births in Suffolk parish registers increased considerably. How to provide for this 'rising' youthful population would become one of the pressing issues in the next decades.[103]

Such changes can be seen in the Sherington family. In the mid-eighteenth century, William Sherington (1690–1752), the husband of Hannah Tink, felt confident enough to describe himself as a 'gentleman' in his will which was embossed with his portrait next to his signature.[104] But for the next generation prospects were not so bright. There is now clear evidence of a family move away from Westleton.

---

102 Ivimey, *Westleton from the 1830s to the 1960s*, 90–91.
103 Dymond and Northeast, *A History of Suffolk*, 96.
104 Yoxford Parish Registers, Suffolk Records Office, Ipswich.

Third son of William the 'gentleman', John Sherington was born in Westleton in 1737. Aged twenty-four, in 1760 he married Ann Reeve at Yoxford. At the virtual centre of 'The Garden of Suffolk', Yoxford is just inland from Westleton. While the name of Westleton is Scandinavian in origin, Yoxford takes its name from a ford across the river, probably a ford wide enough to be passable by 'a yoxen abreast'. The two villages had developed close relations from the medieval period, both being part of the local granges of Sibton Abbey. But Yoxford already had two substantial manors before the Norman conquest. In the Domesday Book there were another five smaller manors.[105]

The Reeve family had been associated with Darsham, the neighbouring village to Yoxford, and had been tenants of the local gentry, John Hopton, in the late fifteenth century.[106] According to the parish registers, John Sherington and his wife Ann (nee Reeve) had twelve children between 1762 and 1785. Six boys – William (1765), John (1765) Thomas (1768) Henry (1776), Robert (1776) and James (1780) – and four girls – Maria (1767) Elizabeth (1767), Sarah (1771) and Ann (1785) – seem to have survived into infancy although perhaps not childhood. As indicated, this high level of fertility was typical of late-eighteenth century Suffolk. But it was difficult to sustain a large family. When John died in 1816 at the age of seventy-nine he had lived a long life for a man then in Suffolk. But already social and economic change made life even more difficult.

The end of the Napoleonic Wars in 1815, the year before John Sherington died, brought the collapse of agricultural prices which had been sustained during a wartime economic boom. Even in 1814, corn prices began to fall, profits were shrinking and men were laid off. By 1816–17 the situation was desperate. Farmers found that land they had bought was not worth the price they

---

105 Norman Scarfe, *Suffolk in the Middle Ages* (Woodbridge: Boydell Press, 1986), 140–55.
106 Richmond, *John Hopton*, 167–68.

had paid. Those leasing could not pay rents. A third of the population was unemployed. Gentlemen formerly of 'comfortable incomes' were now unable to pay bills; farmers once accustomed to eating at the local inn had to walk home to dinner. While Northern England industrialised, East Anglia became impoverished. Suffolk now spent one pound per head each year on relief for the 'poor', Lancashire spent only one quarter of that amount. Even the old cottage industries of combing wool and spinning yarn were ruined by the competition from the Northern spinning mills. In the wake of the Napoleonic Wars, Parliament enacted the Corn Laws imposing duties on imported food as a desperate but futile effort to save rural England.[107]

In the 1820s, William Cobbett, a farmer gentleman from Surrey, began a number of tours on horseback throughout Southern England, seeking to record and understand the changes overcoming old rural communities now being absorbed into the expanding urban and industrial centres. He later published his findings as *Rural Rides*. Of the Suffolk countryside and Suffolk farmers, he wrote an elegy which reflected the past as much as the present:

> you can, in no direction, go ... a quarter of a mile without finding views that a painter might crave, and the country ... so well cultivated; the land in such a beautiful state, the farmhouses all so white, and all so much alike; the barns, and everything about the homesteads so smug; the stocks of turnips so abundant everywhere; the sheep and cattle in such fine order; the wheat all drilled; the ploughman so expert; the furrows, if a quarter of a mile long, as straight as a line, and laid as truly as if with a level; in short, here is everything to delight the eye; and to make the people proud of this county. I have always found Suffolk farmers great boasters of their superiority over others; and I must say that it is not without reason ...

107 Dymond and Northeast, *A History of Suffolk*, 97–99.

> I remarked that I did not see in the whole county one single instance of paper rags supplying the place of glass in any window, and did not see one miserable hovel in which a labourer resided.[108]

This was an elegant epitaph for a way of life already dying. For the three decades after 1815 Suffolk was actually a county of desperation and social unrest often involving violence and political action. Following the 1834 English Poor Law, the new Poor Law Commissioners had powers to assist migration. Many left Suffolk migrating to London and even beyond. By the late 1830s, there were more migrants being assisted from Suffolk than any other county in Britain. Most crossed the Atlantic to the Americas where migrants from Suffolk had settled since the seventeenth century. A small few were transported as convicts to Australia, following the rural unrest and burning of hay 'ricks' in the 1830s. Some even departed Suffolk for the Antipodes as assisted migrants, particularly from the coastal areas near Westleton.[109]

In Westleton itself, at least one family was assisted out of local parish rates to emigrate to Canada in 1845.[110] At the 1851 census, there were almost 1000 inhabitants in the village, with 205 occupied houses and ten empty dwellings. But the decline in the population was already underway with the continuing drift away to local market towns, such as Wickham Market, or to non-agricultural work such as labourers on the expanding railways. Westleton in the mid-nineteenth century reflected much of the past rather than hopes for the future. Two-thirds of the population in 1851 had been born in the village, and most of the rest came from nearby villages or at least from within Suffolk.[111]And to judge from the grave stones still standing in the St Peter's

---

108 William Cobbett, *Rural Rides*, 1830, cited in Richard Tames, *Anglian Images* (Stroud: Allan Sutton, 1991), 114, 118.
109 James Jupp (ed.), *Encyclopædia of the Australia People* (Sydney: Angus & Robertson, 1989), 390–91.
110 Ivimey, *Westleton*, 51.

graveyard at the end of the twentieth century a few Sheringtons had remained in the village until at least the late nineteenth century.

By the twentieth century, the Suffolk coast still retained parts of its rural past but now attracted those who would visit for holidays or who had come to live because of the attractions of the sea and walks. In the 1930s, Suffolk-born Julian Tennyson, a great-great-grandson of the Poet Laureate Alfred Tennyson, still celebrated the farmers, sea farers, environment, and life of Suffolk, particularly along that specific part of the coast just near the Minsmere Cliffs:

> It is a country that you must walk in, get lost in, whose loveliness is rich, wild and changeful ... This is England's last offering; she can take you no farther, and farther you do not want to go ... The heaths here, known as the Westleton Heaths – a name which always suggests to me poke-bonnets and Victorian Valentines – are the grandest I have ever seen.[112]

111 Ibid.,14–18. See also Frank Grace 'Population Trends, 1811–1981' in David Dymond and Edward Martin (eds), *An Historical Atlas of Suffolk* (Ipswich: Suffolk County Council, 1988), 80.

112 Julian Tennyson, *Suffolk Scene* (London: Blackie and Son, 1939), 180. Born in 1915, Tennyson enlisted on the outbreak of war in 1939 and was killed in Burma in 1945. He is buried at St Botolph Church in the village of Iken across from the marshes of Snape Malting near Aldeburgh.

Bruce Sherington at the village of Sharrington, Norfolk, 1990.

Sutton Hoo burial mounds, 1990. On the left in the distance is Helen Sherington, wife of Bruce Sherington.

Dunwich Beach.

Gregory Sherington in front of the ruins of Greyfriars Monastery, Dunwich, 1991.

Once a Roman path through Dunwich Heath, now the road to Westleton.

Entering the village of Westleton from Dunwich.

Bruce Sherington at Westleton, 1990.

Gregory Sherington at Westleton village green, 1991.

The 'Balmayes' fields acquired by Thomas Sherington in 1536 and described in his will of 1552.

St Peter's Church, Westleton.

Westleton fields.

The 'Lamb Pits', Westleton – family land described by Thomas Sherington in his will of 1638.

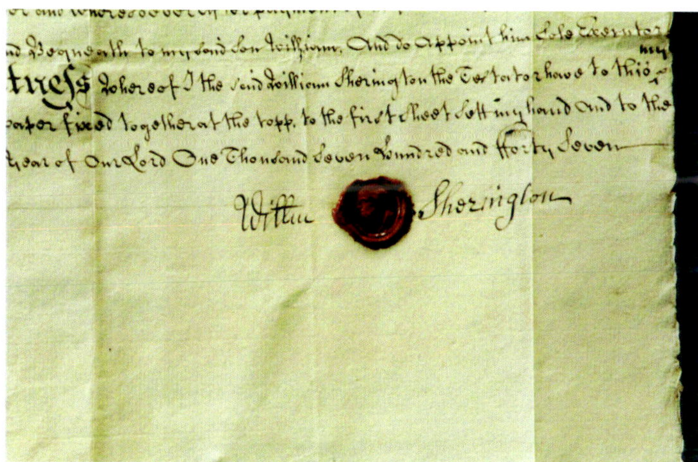

...and Bequeath to my said Son William, And do appoint him Sole Executor
my
...tness whereof I the said William Sherington the Testator have to this
paper fixed together at the topp. to the first sheet sett my hand and to the
year of our Lord One Thousand Seven Hundred and Forty Seven

Willm Sherington

In 1747 William Sherington, 'gentleman', embossed his signed will with his own portrait in wax.

William and Hannah Sherington's headstones, still joined together after more than 250 years.

The village of Yoxford, the 'garden' of Suffolk.

Robert Sherington in 1990, before St Peter's Church, Westleton, where Sheringtons over six generations were married, baptised and buried.

The village of Wickham Market, a place of rural manufacture.

II
South London and Beyond

Lo! Norwood's prescient tribe appears.
From yonder groupe beneath the tree
Of youth in sylvan revelry,
To hear the tidings fate reveals,
A lovley maiden slily steals . . .
A gypsey poring o'er her hand,
In solemn conference they stand . . . ;
Love's soft confessions bright'ning lie,
And whisper in her dewy eye;
There the deep Sybil reads her part,
And frames a case to reach the heart,
Of faith, unrival'd by the dove,
Of sighs, tears, vows, – the words of love;
Of bow'rs of bliss, and lasting joys,
Not winter kills, or Time Destroys;
Ah credulous, the system leave,
For what we wish we soon believe

Samuel Howell, 'Norwood' [1820] cited in John Coulter, *Norwood Past* (London: Coulter Publications, 1996), 11–12.

Upper Norwood

During the nineteenth century London became a centre of attraction for new settlers from the southern and eastern counties of England. Many left East Anglia and nearby areas seeking new opportunities in the capital. By the mid-nineteenth century over 300 000 internal migrants from south-east England were living in the London area and over half of these were women obviously drawn by work in domestic service or in the shops and commercial centres.[1] London became a metropolitan web drawing in and stretching out to capture new settlers and older settlements.

The life of central London was captured in the prose of that great narrator of the capital Charles Dickens.[2] Dickens had lived part of his early life on the edge of the capital in Rochester Kent where he would later return to end his days and write his last novel. Outer London in the early nineteenth century was not yet part of the crowded metropolis it was to become a century later. On the fringes of the capital was still a collection of semi-rural settlements. South London was a place of villages and woods where gypsies supposedly gathered. In the seventeenth century, Samuel Pepys' wife used to journey out from London to converse with these gypsies of the 'North Wood' later to become 'Norwood'. Early-nineteenth-century migration was thus not always a move into an urban setting. Rather, some migrants from Suffolk and other counties were often moving closer to central London but still into semi-rural contexts that provided new opportunities, some of which were not necessarily even semi-industrial despite the growing effect of the industrial revolution particularly in the North of England. For in the end London was a capital of commerce and consumption and all that went with such forms of production and enjoyment. And this was also emphasised in

1 Dudley Baines, *Migration in a Mature Economy: Emigration and Internal Migration in England and Wales* (Cambridge: Cambridge University Press, 1985), 162.
2 Claire Tomalin, *Charles Dickens: A Life* (London: Penguin, 2003).

the settlements on the periphery of the capital. Eventually the population would spread to as well as out from the metropolitan centre, journeying on the new railways, to create suburbs such as Camberwell which soon embraced districts close to the city as well as the more salubrious heights of South London around Dulwich. The old rural estates and manors were broken up to build new housing estates for the expanding population which would 'commute' by rail into London.[3]

Migration to the outskirts of the capital was part of the transition of nineteenth-century Britain into the first society built on capitalism, industrialisation and urbanisation. And this helped to create middle-class families with new values and outlooks. The life of the yeomanry had centred on land and agricultural production and communal village life. The family life of the urban middle class was more focused on private affairs, including religion, often evangelical or non-conformist, in contrast to the traditional Anglican faith of much of rural Suffolk. Many of the nineteenth-century middle class were establishing a family business. There were due and 'separate spheres' for men to run the business and women to maintain the family household.[4]

The Sheringtons from Suffolk were part of this social and cultural change. They had originated mainly as yeomen farmers founded on landed enterprise. The transformation of life in the creation of the nineteenth-century city increasingly based on suburbs brought forth different forms of making a living. Almost in the ways if not the manner of the South London gypsies, Henry Sherington was of those sojourners from rural Suffolk who for personal and religious purposes came to find new opportunities on the fringes of London. Born in 1776, Henry was the sixth born son of John Sherington, formerly of Westleton, and

3 H.J. Dyos, *Victorian Suburb: A Study of the Growth of Camberwell* (Leicester: Leicester University Press, 1959).

4 Leonore Davidoff and Catherine Hall, *Family Fortunes: Men and Women of the English Middle Class, 1780–1850* (Chicago: University of Chicago Press, 1991).

Ann Reeve of Yoxford. Lack of opportunity may have turned him away from the family tradition of farming although his younger brother James, born in 1780, married and stayed in Yoxford producing five daughters before he died in 1835. Henry would follow a different path.

In 1805 Henry Sherington married Charlotte Winter of Cookley parish, Suffolk, where there had once been the manor of Sibton Abbey which had been the landlord for parts of Westleton. The new couple moved to Wickham Market not far from Yoxford. Situated on the borders of woodland and sand districts of Suffolk, a place of settlement since the era of the Romans, and a market town since the fourteenth century, Wickham Market had become a growing industrial and commercial centre with an iron works established in 1780.[5]

Henry and Charlotte had at least seven children of whom at least four survived infancy – Robert (1807), Sarah (1812) Matilda (1813) and Charles (1814). All these children were baptised in the local Church of England in Wickham Market. But two later-born daughters – Charlotte (1816) and Betsy (1824) – were baptised in the local Methodist chapel in Framlingham and Peasenhall, close to Yoxford.[6]

The shift to the Methodist Chapel reflected a general pattern of religious revival in England. The period from 1790 to 1840 was one of a 'great upsurge of nonconformity' across Suffolk and other parts of England. By the religious census of 1851 almost one-third of those attending Sunday service in the county did so in a chapel rather than a church with many nonconformists being Methodists.[7] It would seem that Henry may have been part of this religious and social movement. If so, he was breaking with the traditions of the earlier Sheringtons who had attended St Peter's, Westleton. But even in Westleton itself Methodists had

5 Jobson, *Suffolk Villages*, 77.
6 Mormon Transcripts, Suffolk Records Office, Ipswich.
7 Dymond and Northeast, *A History of Suffolk*, 110–11.

a hold by the early nineteenth century with a chapel at nearby Middleton and by 1832 also at Westleton itself which was on the local Peasenhall preachers' circuit.[8] Overall, East Anglia, and specifically Essex and Suffolk, were by 1851 part of a regional band from the Midlands to the South East which formed 'the religious cockpit of England'. [9]

Henry Sherington and his family were part of that religious cockpit. The traditions of evangelical religious nonconformity from Suffolk were retained even when the family moved to London. In 1835, Henry's son Charles, then in his early 20s, wrote to his parents from Yoxford where he was staying with cousins. Charles took the opportunity to reflect on the Christian commitment of his grandmother Ann (nee Reeve), 'a deep and Genuine piety', as well as on the earlier family associations with Framlingham chapel. Charles himself looked forward to the 'eternal glory' which he believed his grandmother now enjoyed. And as part of his faith he attended a 'love feast' in the local chapel. It was sign of his emerging evangelical faith.[10]

But the early nineteenth century was not just a period of changing religious commitments. There was also a search for new occupations in new urban environments. Henry Sherington's occupation as a 'hairdresser' is a case in point. The occupation of 'hairdresser' apparently emerged in eighteenth-century Europe as one concerned with the preparation of wigs and then with attention to natural hair as 'polite society' surrendered artificial wigs for nature's own. More generally the 'hairdresser' was probably an occupation soon meeting middle-class concern for dress and appearance. Henry Sherington was now part of the semi-urban middle class and his livelihood depended on their consumption and patronage.

---

8 Ivimey, *Westleton from the 1830s to the 1960s*, 57.
9 Davidoff and Hall, *Family Fortunes*, 80.
10 Letter, Charles Sherington to 'Dear Parents', 23 May 1835 (courtesy of Mark Shephard).

Knowing one's ancestors becomes much easier from the records created during the nineteenth century. National registration of births, deaths and marriages from 1837 virtually supplanted the older form of parish records. Using indexes to these registration records has provided a way of tracing families. This has been made much easier with digitisation. From 1841 there was also a national census of the population held every ten years, recorded through a survey depending on where someone was residing on a particular day. After a century the census became publically available, providing further details on such matters as individuals' occupations, where they were residing, and the size of their families. Over forty years of research into birth, death and marriage certificates and national census data form a part of the following discussion. (There are no specific reference details for these sources in footnotes but the records of national registration of birth, deaths and marriages and the national census can now be accessed online).

At the 1841 census Henry Sherington was recorded as living in Norwood on the southern outskirts of London. As this was the first national census it may be that he had come to Norwood much earlier. Certainly, Norwood was still emerging from its rural past. An 1826 directory had listed twenty shops. By 1845 there were about forty trades in 128 shops with a great number of specialities in such areas as watch makers, a chemist and druggist, stationers and a pastry cook.[11] Thus the uncle of Charles Dickens on his mother's side, John Barrow, had come to live in Norwood where his nephew Charles often visited him (Barrow later employed the young Dickens as a reporter).[12] Not just middle-class commerce but also middle-class suburbia had begun to arrive in Norwood by the mid-nineteenth century and the Sherington family was part of it.

---

11 John Coulter, *Norwood Past* (London: Coutler Publications, 1996), 69.

12 Tomalin, *Charles Dickens: A Life*, 48–51.

Aged sixty-five at the 1841 census, Henry was living with his son Charles, and his youngest daughter Betsy, aged fifteen. A year later, in 1842, Charles married Mary Short Cottom from Holbeach in Lincolnshire – another example of the move from East Anglia into London. Charles had followed his father's occupation as a 'hairdresser' and was also residing in Norwood. In this way skills and enterprise were handed down from one generation to another. So it seems was the tradition of religious nonconformity – not so much as a expression of religious dissent but as a form of moral respectability which justified enterprise in this life in order to secure the next.

The name of Norwood was 'drawn' from the Great North Wood, a natural oak forest which formed a wilderness on the southern edge of the ever expanding metropolis of London. Over the centuries the wood had become 'the centre and unifying feature' of settlements all around – villages, hamlets and isolated farms and the gypsies. The transformation of this wooded rural area began in the mid-eighteenth century when Parliament legislated for the enclosure of commons, open fields and woods across England. Much of this denied small farmers traditional rights and allowed larger property holders to consolidate. In South London, it was now possible to enclose land into smaller plots which could be sold to an expanding urban population. In the Norwood area, this process occurred from the 1790s to the 1820s. The large allotments arising out of these enclosures were placed on the high ground, providing for middle-class villas on the heights of Upper Norwood, and the smaller allotments in the valleys for the working class and poor.[13]

By the 1830s, Norwood was described in a guide as 'a village situated on the outskirts of an extensive wood, and long famed for the salubrity of its air, and the beauty of its surrounding

13 Coulter, *Norwood*, 28–40.

scenery, with smiling villas and blooming flower gardens'.[14] While Norwood was still distant from London, many new middle-class settlers came from the City in the period 1800 to 1840, including bankers, solicitors and merchants.[15] It was a place for pleasure and home living. Nearby Beulah spa was opened in 1831 and was apparently designed for locals and commuters from London. In 1845, *Punch* described the spa setting with beautiful gardens, lawns, grottoes, hermitages and kiosks.[16]

Henry Sherington died on 16 April 1852 of bronchitis and complications. Aged seventy-six, he was then residing at 1 Lutheran Place Upper Tulse Hill in the Brixton Parish of Lambton in the county of Surrey along with his daughter Betsy who had now married Henry Worsley from Surrey. His son and daughter-in-law, Charles and Mary Sherington, now had a growing family and apparently a thriving business, all within the atmosphere of religious piety. William Charles was the first born in 1842 followed by (Mary) Jane in 1847, Anne (Annie) in 1849, Helen (soon known as 'Nellie') in about 1853 and finally Charles in 1855.

Evangelical Christianity was often the foundation of the mid-nineteenth-century middle-class family life in Britain. Religion helped to define roles based on gender. As head of the household a middle-class father often led the family in prayer and even oversaw the observance of other religious practice such as the reading of Scripture. While men assumed the leading role in passing on the faith, wives and daughters were assigned a role of protecting the moral virtue of the family.[17]

In the Sherington family Charles Sherington senior had a reputation of being a 'Godly man'. A photo survives of a well-dressed patriarch with his hand on the Bible – a sign perhaps

14 Alan Warwick, *The Phoenix Suburb* (London: Blue Boar Press, 1982), 61.

15 Coulter, *Norwood*, 41–53.

16 Warwick, *The Phoenix Suburb*, 69.

17 Davidoff and Hall, *Family Fortunes*, 107–18.

of being a Methodist lay preacher. Although he did not pass on his 'trade' of hairdresser to his first born there was the continuing tradition of the lay preacher which his son William Charles would assume intermittently in adult life.

With moral respectability came comfort if not wealth. The nineteenth-century street directories indicate that from at least 1865 Charles Sherington was living at 'Codrington Villa', Central Hill Upper Norwood. The house was near the junction of Central Hill and Gipsy Hill, and very close to the Methodist chapel which was originally located on Gipsy Hill. (Central Hill was one of the main thoroughfares through Upper Norwood while houses on Gipsy Hill had views across South London to St Paul's Cathedral.) 'Codrington Villa' has since been destroyed along with neighbouring properties, replaced by a set of bland late-twentieth-century 'social housing'. But in the late nineteenth century the Sherington family continued to live around the area, owning houses on Gipsy Hill itself. At least two of these houses still stand.

When Charles Sherington died in 1868 there was public notice of his passing with the middle-class practice of funeral cards dressed in black. A solid gravestone, commemorating Charles and later his wife Mary, was erected in the West Norwood extensive graveyard, although the memorial is now apparently broken up or lost with the ravages of time.[18] Nor apparently did he leave his wife and family in genteel poverty. Almost thirty years after he died he was still described as a man of 'independent means' on the marriage certificate of his daughter Jane.[19]

18 Copies of funeral card and photo of gravestone and other information courtesy of Mark Shephard.
19 Copy of marriage certificate courtesy of Mark Shephard.

The Crystal Palace

In the mid-1850s Norwood and its surrounding hamlets were transformed by the construction of a new vast edifice. Prince Albert, the consort of Queen Victoria, had urged the British Government to create an Exhibition in Hyde Park in Central London. This led to the building of the famous Crystal Palace as a showpiece of British design and as a way to show off British products. Following the 1851 Exhibition in Hyde Park, the government decided to transfer the Crystal Palace to a more permanent site at Norwood – a People's Palace for culture, art and design and commerce. Its reconstruction provided opportunities for individuals and families to take up stalls to display and sell goods – an indication of the adage of the British as a nation of shopkeepers. At the same time, there would be pleasure gardens and eventually musical and other performances:

> If the Great Exhibition was a microcosm of Victorian industry then the Sydenham Crystal Palace was one of Victorian leisure. At a time when museums, galleries and parks were few it offered Londoners the opportunity to expand their knowledge of the world while relaxing in lovely surroundings. They could contemplate the splendid rural view of Kent and Surrey, ponder on the monsters that towered amongst the trees, picnic in the woods or on the lawns– and all within a few minutes' journey from centre of the city.[20]

Norwood and surrounding suburbs now became a very desirable place to live. To bring sightseers and serve new commuters, a new railway station was opened, designed by Charles Barry the former architect of the parliamentary buildings at Westminster (and father of Alfred Barry, public school headmaster, educationist and later Bishop of Sydney in the 1880s). As a sign of

20 Patrick Beaver, *The Crystal Palace* (London: Phillimore, 1986), 99.

the new age, Beulah Spa closed in 1856 unable to compete with the new wonders of the Crystal Palace which also had its own fountains and gardens.[21] It was an indication that Norwood was now becoming less of an outpost and more of a London suburb. Property developers moved in to create new suburban estates. Between 1852 and 1854, fifty middle-class houses were built. Another estate adjacent to the Crystal Palace was Dulwich Wood which Charles Barry and his son created from the late 1850s.[22] By the 1860s the old Norwood was being divided up between the new boroughs of Croydon, Lambeth, Southwark and Bromley.[23]

Crystal Palace and Norwood even attracted international interest. Escaping the Franco-Prussian War, the French impressionist Camille Pissarro came to live at Norwood in 1870–72. Overall he produced thirteen oil paintings and various water colours in these two years. His paintings of the Crystal Palace and Norwood now form an important part of the collections of major galleries and private collections throughout the world. Many of his fellow impressionists such as Cezanne regard Pissarro's work in the 1870s as the pinnacle of the Impressionist movement for that period. He captured the suburban transition of South London and, in painting the Crystal Palace, less than twenty years old, showed how the Impressionists were prepared to depict modern buildings. [24]

The Crystal Palace was thus both the symbol and focus of this new suburban world of South London. Its architect, James Paxton, previously the landscape architect for Chatsworth House, home of Lord Derby, had built a palace for the people from iron and glass reflecting what British industry could achieve in the mid-Victorian era. The engineer Brunel had designed two grand north and south towers to supply water to the fountains in the

21 Warwick, *The Phoenix Suburb*, 69–70.
22 Coulter, *Norwood*, 94–107.
23 Ibid., 108.
24 Nicholas Reed, *Camille Pissarro at Crystal Palace* (London: Lilburne Press, 1995), 2–3.

gardens. Centrepiece of the palace would the great Handel organ and the hall for music festivals. Overall, it was a place for pleasure and profit, in so keeping with the values of the new suburban middle class, with stalls for commerce being given a place along with the displays of wonders from the world. When Queen Victoria opened the Crystal Palace in 1854, some even regarded the iron and glass structure as already the eighth wonder of the world; when fire destroyed the palace in 1936 Winston Churchill was said to have stood by with tears on his face constantly muttering, 'This is an end of an age'.[25]

Amongst the new settlers attracted to South London because of the Crystal Palace were the Banfields.[26] In some ways the Banfields were similar to the Sheringtons as recent settlers in London, except that commerce was probably long in the family's veins. Born in Taunton Somerset about 1823, the son of Samuel Banfield, nominated on the birth certificate as 'a shopkeeper' but in effect a 'china dealer', Henry Banfield had probably moved to London in the early 1840s. At the 1841 census Henry was listed as an accountant aged fifteen. On 22 August 1848 in the parish church of Corfe Somerset, Henry Banfield married a local girl named Jane Wilcox, aged about twenty-three, the daughter of a servant, Robert Wilcox. Henry was then living at 18 Regents Street London and still describing his occupation as 'accountant'.

By the census of 1851 the Banfields had a one-year-old son named Henry. As noted below, this may have become 'Harry' Banfield (so distinguishing him from his father). The Banfield residence was then at 32 Halsley Road, Chelsea. The house still stands as part of a uniform street of early-nineteenth-century houses on each side. Henry Banfield was now a 'clerk' with Alfred Bainbridge and Richard Percival Daniell 'china men by special

---

25 Beaver, *The Crystal Palace*, 69–148; Warwick, *The Phoenix Suburb*, 151, 252.

26 William Fullick and Margaret Byrne have carried out much of the recent research on the residences of Banfield and have also confirmed the Banfields' living arrangements as revealed at the various censuses.

appointment to Her Majesty'. The firm was located at 129 New Bond Street and was quite obviously a business of some status and standing.

On 18 September 1852, Henry's and Jane's daughter Ada Caroline was born; the birth was registered in the district of St George Hanover Square and as informant Henry indicated that he was still a commercial clerk residing at 129 New Bond Street. All this would suggest that Henry Banfield from Somerset, son of china merchant Samuel, had soon established himself in an important china merchant house in central London and was living in fashionable areas such as Chelsea and Regent Street. It may have been that he had resided at his place of employment for a while but this is less likely considering he had a growing family.

By the 1860s, a domestic change had come over the lives of Henry and Jane Banfield. They had moved from the West End of London to Sydenham Hill near Crystal Palace and Upper Norwood and were living in 'Hermitage Villa' at 176 Wells Road: a house site which no longer seems to exist. Henry now described himself as a 'china dealer' living with his wife Jane and daughters Ada, now aged eight, and Clara aged six. There was also in the household an apprentice china dealer William Hawkins aged seventeen and Esther Voucher aged twenty-two, who was possibly a house servant. At the 1871 census there was still a live-in house servant suggesting that the Banfield family had attained some form of middle-class affluence.

While the Banfields were living near Crystal Palace there is no clear evidence that Henry had established a chinaware business there. There was no indication in the 1860s and 1870s of Henry advertising his wares in either local newspapers or trade and other directories. Nor is there any clear evidence that he operated a business from home or had established separate business premises. It may be that Henry Banfield remained an employee of the china dealers in London, or even had become a partner in the firm, commuting to London by train. What is clear is that he now occupied substantial homes in the Crystal Palace area.

By the 1870s he was resident and perhaps owner of two substantial houses at 3–4 Palace Grove, Penge, occupying each of them at different points in time. [27] These were not far from the Crystal Palace. And there was now a third daughter: Alice who was aged eight in 1871.

Whatever the nature of the business of the Banfields, they soon came into contact with the Sheringtons. In 1867, the year before her father died and on her eighteenth birthday, Annie Sherington, daughter of Charles, began to keep a diary. The diary covered the period 1867–68, and then was intermittently written in until 1871. Much of it was filled with matters of religion and Church perhaps reflecting the ways of her father. There were also references to social contacts and acquaintances particularly at the Crystal Palace where Annie and others had a 'counter'. Perhaps this was the way the Sheringtons and Banfields met. By 1868 there were references to social occasions involving members of the Sherington and Banfield families.[28] Of most significance, William Charles Sherington, the brother of Annie, became involved with the Banfields. By the 1870s, William Charles Sherington, eldest in the family, was in his late 20s. There is some suggestion that he was finding it difficult to 'settle down'. William appears to have been away from home for most of this period, departing on Mondays and returning on Saturdays. At the time of his father's death in July 1868 he was summoned by telegram and arrived just in time to read the Bible and pray with his father. In January 1870 a reference in Annie's diary indicated that

> William came home very ill. He had been put into a damp bed & and we scarcely thought he would be able to get about again. After some time we saw an amendment. Mother nursed him

27 Based on the research of William Fullick and Margaret Byrne.
28 Annie Sherington, Diary (courtesy of Mark Shephard).

> day and night. I often wonder she did not get knocked up, but when God sends a trial, He sends grace to help us bear it.[29]

Throughout the early 1870s the Sheringtons and Banfields appear to come closer together. Family, home and church or chapel provided much of the foundations for these social contacts. On one occasion Annie recorded in her diary that on Easter Sunday 'Went to tea at Mr Banfields with Janie and Charlie. William had been there all day. In the evening went and heard Mr Silcox at Sydenham. William, Ada, Clara and I went with Charlie' – supposedly a church occasion to hear a preacher. From September to November 1870 Annie recorded a number of walks with the Banfield sisters Ada and Clara. William is also caught up with Sunday school work – so on 16 October 'William went over to Sydenham to give the address' – perhaps at the local Methodist church.[30]

According to the 1871 census Henry Banfield was resident in Palace Crescent, Penge but there is no indication in the census return that his wife Jane was living with him. This suggests that she may have died – and thus may explain why Annie had indicated in her diary cited above that she 'Went to dinner at Mr Banfields' with no reference to Mrs Banfield.[31]

Relations between the Banfields and Sheringtons developed apace in the early 1870s. On 10 September 1873 at St Paul's church, Penge, William Charles Sherington, then aged thirty, and resident at Central Hill Upper Norwood (probably 'Codrington Villa') married Ada Caroline Banfield aged twenty-one, resident at Palace Grove, Penge. William described his occupation as 'merchant' while his father-in-law Henry Banfield, nominated also as a 'merchant', acted as witness for his son-in-law's signature, suggesting a close relation between father-in-law and son-

29 Ibid.
30 Ibid.
31 Annie Sherington, Diary (courtesy of Mark Shephard).

in-law. Ada and William then spent a honeymoon down on the coast at Felixstowe in Suffolk, the groom telling his sister Annie, 'It is a lovely place and I think the change will do us both good, and think when we return to Lordship Lane (in Norwood) you will hardly know us'.[32]

The Pretty Family

The wedding of William Charles Sherington to Ada Banfield was soon matched by the marriage of his sister Annie in a manner that would both tie the Sherington family back to the Suffolk past as well as provide new prospects for extended family opportunities.

In the early 1870s William Pretty became friends with the Sherington family. The Pretty family came from Suffolk. In the late eighteenth century there were many parish register entries for 'Pretty' in the village of Yoxford where Henry Sherington had been born.[33] William Pretty senior was born in Bacton, Suffolk in around 1812. He was the eldest son of a woollen draper and tailor. The family was nonconformist and Wesleyan in faith reflecting the early-nineteenth-century link between religion and business enterprise. More generally their prominence from the mid-nineteenth century was part of the 're-industrialisation' of Suffolk. The old cloth trade of the Middle Ages had declined well before the nineteenth century. In 1849, Suffolk was described as a county 'solely without manufactures'.[34] The new Suffolk industries of the nineteenth century were often associated with agriculture or rural production such as brewing, or agricultural

32 Letter, William Charles to Annie Sherington, September 1871 (courtesy of Mark Shephard).

33 Yoxford Parish registers, Suffolk Records Office, Ipswich.

34 Christine Clarke and Roger Munting, *Suffolk Enterprises: A Guide to the County's Companies and their Historical Records* (Norwich: Centre of East Anglian Studies, n.d.), 10.

implements or engineering. But there was also the growth of substantial industries making 'ready-made' garments for the domestic and even overseas markets.[35]

The Pretty family opportunity for fortunes came in the area of women's clothing and underwear. Suffolk had a reputation for 'bodice making' from at least the seventeenth century. By the mid-nineteenth century, it was already an extensive industry in Ipswich. About 1820, the drapers and silk merchants Footman, Pretty and Nicolson was founded. Reputedly, William Pretty senior bought the 'goodwill' of a corset-making concern from a woman who claimed to be the 'purveyor' to Queen Victoria. In keeping with much early industrial practice the work of producing garments was 'farmed' out to the 'cottage industry' of women working mainly by hand. William Pretty senior apparently saw this as principally an annexe to his main business as a draper.[36]

William Pretty's son William was born in 1842 in Ipswich. After attending the Wesley College, Sheffield he joined his father's business. By 1871 William junior aged twenty-nine, and his wife Margaret, aged thirty-four, were living 'above the shop' at 'Ipswich St Mary At the Tower' along with their children William, aged four, Maud, two, and Ernest just born. On that 1871 census night there were also recorded a large number of 'draper's assistants' on the premises. These employees were perhaps working in the evening, including the fifteen-year-old 'Charlie Sherington', the younger brother of William Charles and Annie. The company for which Charlie was working was now known as Footman, Pretty and Nicolson 'Stay Manufacturers'. Occupying a very large site the company was involved as drapers, silk mercers, warehousemen as well as manufacturing.[37]

---

35 Ibid., 13–14.

36 Page, *The Victorian County History of the Counties of England*, 276. See also Clark and Manning, *Suffolk Enterprises*, 97–99.

37 Information on Prettys courtesy of Mark Shephard and research of Roger Kennell, Hadleigh Suffolk.

Charlie Sherington's employment may have opened up the relationship between the Prettys and Sheringtons. There is also the possibility that Annie met William Pretty through his first wife Margaret (nee Woollard). In June 1871, Annie recorded her in the diary

> Handel Festival Week. Mrs Pearce and Mrs Pretty came and stayed. Mrs Pearce went home Saturday 24 June, Mrs Pretty the 27th. We also had Mr Pretty . . . Mrs Pretty is quite a favourite of mine. I like her much. Charlie was also home for a day or two.[38]

And then on Sunday 25 June Annie records, 'Went to dinner at Mr Banfield's . . . In the afternoon went to school and to tea with Ada. In the evening Mrs Pretty, Ada, William and I went for a walk'.[39]

The Mrs Pretty referred to above was thus possibly Margaret (nee Woollard) the daughter of a Methodist minister and first wife of William Pretty junior. A few months later she died in childbirth following confinement for the birth of her third child. William moved back to live with his parents, with his deceased wife's sister Anne Woollard acting as housekeeper. William now begun to court Annie Sherington. As a potentially 'remarrying man', with two young sons, William pursued Annie, still residing in Norwood, in a nine month courtship revealed through a series of over fifty letters which he wrote from Ipswich followed by visits to London.[40] Part of William's wooing of Annie involved him tantalising her with the prospect of marriage and then in serious jest

38 Annie Sherington, Diary.

39 Ibid.

40 Steven King and Mark Shephard, 'Courtship and the Remarrying Man in Late Victorian England', *Journal of Family History*, July 2012, 37(4), 319–40.

suggesting they would have to live a modest life like a tradesman.[41]

William Pretty married Annie Sherington in June 1874. By the census of 1881, William, aged 39 and still described as a 'draper', was living with Annie (aged thirty-one) along with his daughter Maud Pretty from the first marriage, and the three children of the second marriage, Hilda, aged five, Bertha, aged three, and Frank, aged two, at 11 Henley Road Ipswich. William and Annie eventually had six children joining the three of William's first marriage.

With his father having only marginal interest in the manufacturing side of the business, William apparently saw the opportunities presented from the 1870s with electricity as a new source of power becoming available for sewing machines.[42] And he looked overseas for manufacturing methods. In 1874, he told Annie,

> I have been involved all day with a New Yorker – the largest maker of German corsets in the world. It isn't matter of trying to sell goods just now. . . I could have taken orders yesterday and today for £10 000.[43]

Here was an opportunity not to be missed. In 1875, the formal partnership between William Pretty and his son on the one hand and Alexander Nicolson and Frederick Footman on the other was dissolved. William Pretty junior was now particularly focused on making a new industrial empire out of modern ways of creating women's corsets. In 1881 a new large corset-manufacturing factory was built on Tower Ramparts in Ipswich. When William Pretty senior died in 1889, William Pretty separated out

---

41 Letter, William (Pretty) to Annie (Sherington), 8 June 1874 (courtesy of Mark Shephard).
42 Page, *The Victorian County History of the Counties of England*, 275.
43 Letter, William (Pretty) to Anne (Pretty), 22 May 1874 (courtesy of Mark Shephard).

the corset manufacturing side of the business from the store of Footman Pretty. William Pretty also dissolved a formal partnership with his two brothers Alfred and Edward and became the sole owner of this corset factory of William Pretty and Sons. The motto of the business, 'Sole Makers for Europe and Colonies of Dr Warner's Coraline Corsets', was an appropriate indication of its scope and reach. William had also created the Ipswich Busk and Steel Company as well as the Ipswich Box Company. The latter was incorporated into the Tower Ramparts factory; the corsets had long been sold in long decorative boxes but now these could be made 'in house'. The production of these cardboard boxes was so extensive that William even chartered steamers to bring the boards direct from the mills to Ipswich docks and thence to Tower Ramparts.[44]

William Pretty's business interests would take him on constant trips into Europe and North America – at least forty in the next four decades. The modern hotel accommodation in Chicago in the 1870s particularly impressed him, telling his wife Annie, 'this place beats' New York hotels into 'fits'.[45] He returned to Chicago on many occasions. He also took a great interest in emerging modern American methods of manufacture and in such areas as the shoe and boot industry where by subdividing the production process efficiencies and improvements could be achieved. Eventually, this would lead to a system of 'outworker' or 'branch' factories in Suffolk and Norfolk where the production process was begun only to be completed at the main factory in Ipswich. The first outworker factory actually opened in Bury St Edmunds in 1887 to be followed by others over the next two decades in such places as Braintree, Great Yarmouth, Hadleigh, Kings Lynn, Stowmarket, Beccles, Sudbury, Witham, and Wood-

---

44 Based on research of Roger Kennell.

45 Letter, William Pretty to Annie Pretty, 4 July 1876 (courtesy of Mark Shephard). He apparently did not realise it but William was in Chicago on the centenary of American Independence Day.

bridge. By the early twentieth century, Suffolk was *the* English county for corsets. At the same time, Pretty soon had a national reputation as a progressive employer providing creches and a dining room for his mainly female workforce which numbered 1200 by the early twentieth century.[46]

While his father had established the family business in partnership, William Pretty exhibited all the characteristics of the sole entrepreneur, owning and managing his own business. Drawing on modern methods, he created a large manufacturing factory, developed a particular William Pretty and Sons brand of corset, and then, most unusually for late-nineteenth-century British entrepreneurs, serving an international market through a world sales strategy. When British manufacturing seemed to be losing out to Germany and America in the late nineteenth century William Pretty and Sons seemed a great success.[47] And all in ways that were seen not to exploit his female workforce but to offer them opportunities for modern factory work along with their responsibilities as mothers.

Of course William Pretty would probably never have considered having his own wife at work. The mid-nineteenth-century middle-class woman might have been found helping out in retail. But Annie Pretty would certainly have given up her counter at the Crystal Palace once she married William. Nor was the factory floor a place for a respectable lady in the late nineteenth century even if most of the workers were female. With her growing family Annie had her own responsibilities of maintaining a family in the ways of moral virtue as her father had taught her, as well as overseeing the running of the family home. Ideas of independence for a wife as well as prospects of wealth had formed part of the correspondence before William and An-

46 Page, *The Victorian County History of the Counties of England*, 276–77.

47 See P.L. Payne, *British Entrepreneurship in the Nineteenth Century* (London: Macmillan, 1988).

nie married. In the end, the latter aim was fulfilled more than the former intent.[48]

And with financial success came personal rewards and new social status. New ways of manufacturing corsets meant that the days of living above the shop were long gone. It was now possible to send his sons Frank and Donald to The Leys, the Methodist English public school near Cambridge. By the 1890s William and Annie were able to move out to a new mansion, 'The Goldrood' on the outskirts of Ipswich, its name soon emblazoned on in the topiary along the path up to the house. He had also established a national profile representing business in the negotiations with Lloyd George over the proposed national unemployment insurance legislation. At the same time, he enjoyed his pleasures particularly figure skating and fox hunting, even combining this latter interest with support for the National Army Reserve for Suffolk. And in this way he was different from his father and the early-nineteenth-century generation of Methodist businessmen who disproved of such 'aristocratic' forms of leisure and pleasure. As William told Annie before their marriage, his father had long opposed him hunting. But William's response even then was that a man of his age, having attained his majority, was entitled to his amusements. Hunting had been his heart's desire since he was young.[49] And now in middle age, with wealth assured, he could indulge himself.

William Pretty had built a family fortune and dynasty based both on an Ipswich factory and international contacts. In contrast, the Sherington family had been now been based in South London in for more than two generations. Some social critics of urban middle-class values, such as Matthew Arnold, believed

48 King and Shephard, 'Courtship and the Re-marrying Man', 12–17.
49 Letter, William Pretty to Annie Sherington, 22 November and 13 December 1873 (courtesy of Mark Shephard).

that suburban living in South London had created 'illiberal dismal lives'.[50] For some members of the Sherington family, circumstances would soon induce them to move on to fields afar, perhaps in an effort to emulate their friend and relative William Pretty.

A Divorce

When William Pretty came to London he often stayed with Ada and William Sherington telling his future wife Annie in October 1873 that the home of the newlyweds could also become a meeting place for them:

> I like Wm's place immensely. It's the jolliest little house at £40 per year I ever saw – we should expect to pay as much for it in Ipswich. It appears to have every convenience and the locality is very pleasant. I've no doubt we shall spend some happy hours there. Ada says that you must always come when in town and I know sufficient of William not to refuse such a good opportunity of meeting you. They appear to get on (as someone would say) 'splendid'.[51]

William and Ada had begun married life at their own residence at 1 Bermuda Villas in Underhill Road (now known as 61 Underhill Road) in what was becoming the fashionable district of Dulwich East (as part of the wider suburb of Camberwell) nearby to Upper Norwood. Underhill Road was near an estate of about eight acres away from Dulwich Park. By the 1870s the estate 'being encircled by modest villa development to the south, and its

---

50 Dyos, *Victorian Suburb*, 192.

51 Letter, William Pretty to Annie Sherington, 9 October 1873 (courtesy of Mark Shephard).

own frontage to Crystal Palace Road had been lined by some groups of semi-detached and terraced villas'.[52]

Here William Henry Sherington was born on 25 September 1874. William Charles proudly sent a telegram to William Pretty in Ipswich, 'At seven o'cock this mng a big boy all well'.[53] But in contrast to the title of 'merchant' on his marriage certificate William Henry now described himself as a 'warehouseman' on his son's birth certificate, an indication perhaps of changing circumstances in his life with consequences for the future. William Charles and Ada Caroline had two more sons – Arthur Charles born in 1876 and John Guy in 1878.

From the late 1870s there are only glimpses in surviving letters of their married life. About 1877, Helen Sherington, sister of Annie, and now known as 'Nellie', wrote to her lover and future husband Steve Thompson including some details of a recent visit to Crystal Palace where the high wind had almost blown off the roof with glass coming down. There was then a meeting in the evening at the Sherington home when 'Mr Banfield, Ada and Will were all here'.[54]

By the late 1870s a crisis had emerged in the lives of William Charles and Ada Caroline Sherington. Almost a century later in 1970 Olive Sherington, the wife of Arthur, the middle of the Sherington boys, indicated to Richard Sherington, the great grandson of Ada Caroline and William Charles Sherington, that much was due to an economic crisis in the family even implying that William Charles had been ultimately responsible.

> Your great-grandparents separated after the collapse of the business (a big glass and china business in Crystal Palace, started by your great-grandmother's father, Mr Banfield). This I

52 Dyos, *Victorian Suburb*, 107.
53 Letter, William Sherington to William Pretty, 25 September 1874 (Sherington Family Papers in possession of authors).
54 Letter, Helen (Sherington) to Steve (Thompson), c.1877 (courtesy of Mark Shephard).

> can tell you, that your great grandmother and her two sisters sold their jewellery and home to pay the creditors in full.[55]

Recent research has thrown into question much of the above.[56] First, as already indicated, there is no clear evidence that Henry Banfield ever had a glass and china business in Crystal Palace. It was only in the 1880s that street directories suggest that a Banfield china business had emerged in the suburb of Sydenham nearby to Crystal Palace. And the formal proprietor was not Henry Banfield, but Clara Banfield his daughter. Now aged in his late fifties, and identified as 'widower' in the 1881 census, Henry was living with Clara, then aged twenty-five, residing at 2 Silverdale Terrrace, Sydenham Road where the china business was located. This address was less fashionable than his house at Palace Grove where Henry had lived a decade earlier. This may suggest that he had fallen on hard times but not even that is certain. Nor can it be assumed that he had an active role in the business Clara ran, although no doubt he would have some role to play.

What is now known, and what Olive Sherington did not reveal, even if she knew, was the dissolution of the marriage of Ada Caroline and William Charles. Civil divorce in England had only been possible since the 1857 Matrimonial Causes Act. Before then, divorce had been only open to men and had to be granted by Act of Parliament. Under the 1857 legislation, a wife could divorce her husband for adultery but also had to prove other faults such as cruelty, rape and incest. But there was still much social sanction against divorce and middle-class women would have only undertaken such a course with some reluctance.

The Civil Divorce Records 1858–1911 for the United Kingdom reveal that Ada Caroline Sherington filed for divorce from

---

55 Letter, Olive Sherington to Richard Sherington, 12 July 1970 (Sherington Family Papers).

56 The following account is based on the research findings of William Fullick and Margaret Byrne.

William Charles Sherington in November 1879. Then living in nearby Beckenham, Ada Caroline stated in her petition to the court that she had lived with her husband at Bermuda Villas and 'divers other places' but was now separated from him. She then claimed: 'The said William Charles Sherington is a man of intemperate habits and has behaved with great violence and cruelty towards me . . . and has frequently struck and assaulted me'. She outlined a number of such assaults over the past two years including throwing her to the ground and throwing her out of the home in her nightdress. The most recent assault had occurred in August 1879 leading to the police intervening and William Charles being sent to prison for seven days and then being 'bound over' to keep the peace. In April 1880 a judicial separation was decreed. Ada Caroline was granted costs of the proceedings and also custody of the three children but no alimony.

For the nineteenth-century middle class in the age of Queen Victoria, divorce was regarded as a social disgrace. There is no doubt that this would have brought great shame on the Sherington name and a particular focus on the character of William Charles Sherington. From the perspective of over a century later it seems to show also the strength and fortitude of Ada Caroline who now fell back on the support of the Banfield family. While Henry was living with his daughter Clara, by the 1881 census Ada Caroline, was recorded as living nearby at 6 Venner Road, Sydenham along with her younger sister Alice now aged eighteen. Two children were recorded in this household – Arthur aged four and a child aged two who was obviously Guy. Ada now described herself as a 'lodgings housekeeper' and there was a twenty-one-year-old female boarding with her. The eldest son of Ada, William Henry, now aged six, was then living in Somerset, perhaps with relatives or friends of Henry.

The overall suburb of Sydenham, like Upper Norwood and Penge, had grown with the establishment of the Crystal Palace and the coming of the railway, so that the population had expanded from just under 3000 in 1841 to over 20 000 in 1871. And Venner Road, where Ada was living in 1881, was near the railway and the palace; even in the early twentieth century the address was regarded as 'quite a select area'.[57] So in this respect, financially Ada seems to have survived the break-up of the marriage.

By 1885, there is also an indication that Ada Caroline was even thinking of a new marriage. Banns of a future marriage in the Church of England were announced between Charles James Malone and Ada Banfield. But there is no evidence that the marriage proceeded. Instead, for much of the mid to late 1880s, Ada Caroline and her sons made a life in Sydenham still near to her family.

William Henry Sherington was now attending Sydenham Hill School established by the School Board for London which had been created as part of the important 1870 Education Act designed to create through local rates and government grants local school board 'national' or non-denominational schools in competition with the longer established 'voluntary' Church schools which also received grants from government. Still surviving is a card awarded to 'William Sherrington' as a scholar, aged eleven, in the fourth standard of the school for 'Punctual and Regular Attendance' for the School Quarter ended June 1885.

By 1888, William Henry, now aged fourteen, had left school and was in the employ of J.G. Atkinson, Late W.R. Wheeler, Chemist and Druggist of Westow Hill Upper Norwood. For a long time, a pharmacy stood on that site which was just along the road from the former Sherington family home of Codrington Villa on Central Hill. On Sundays, William and his brother Arthur were choir boys at St Paul's Upper Norwood where they also participated in other activities such as cricket matches.[58]

57 Doris E. Pullen, *Sydenham* (London: self-published, 1974), 2, 23.
58 Sydenham School Board for London Card, 1885; Reference from Choirmaster, St Paul's Upper Norwood, 2 August 1888 (Sherington Family Papers).

As for William Charles Sherington, by the mid-1880s he had left England forever.

Westward Ho

From the mid-1850s to the early 1890s about eight million of the population of Britain and Ireland, adults and children, left for destinations outside Europe. Two-thirds went to the United States of America, about a tenth to Canada and just over one-sixth to Australasia. The British began to people the world:

> The British people became a global people in the late nineteenth century. It was an extraordinarily open world in which British capital, trade and their accompanying personnel reached into practically every country in the world. Some were career migrants, planters, administrators and missionaries, to whom may be added to all the technicians and managers who were indispensable to the imperial economy, formal and informal. Mass emigration from the British Isles was directed mostly to the United States and Canada and to the thinly lands expropriated by imperial Britain in Australasia.[59]

From the 1870s, with the advent of the steam ship, the sea journey became less arduous and about half had left with the intention of returning, particularly if they had gone to North America for seasonal labouring work. Whereas in the early nineteenth century much of the migration from Britain was family groups from rural counties which were often in economic and social decline, such as Suffolk, by the late nineteenth century the pattern was more generally young adult migrants from urban areas. More

59 Eric Richards, *Britannia's Children: Emigration from England Scotland, Wales and Ireland* (London: Hambledon and London, 2004), 175.

than one-third of the permanent emigrants from the 1860s onwards came from London, the West Midlands or Lancashire.[60]

There was a growing push for Londoners to go abroad. Urbanisation in nineteenth-century Britain often disturbed traditional patterns of family associations while providing limited opportunities for permanent work, affecting both men and women. Single female migrants now constituted over one-third of all emigrants between 1860 and 1900, with no less than one-fifth of all female emigrants in these years having been born in London.[61]

The 1880s was *the* decade of leaving London for overseas to America or the Empire of settlement. Overall, about 500 000 of the English and Welsh population emigrated in the 1860s, and the same numbers again in the 1870s, but in the 1880s, 800 000 or 3.1 per cent of the total population left rarely to return.[62] The explanation for this 'migration boom' can be partly understood through the usual 'push' and 'pull' of economic as well as social and individual causes. Despite the success of such businessmen as William Pretty, with his corsets sold to the world, from the mid-1870s to the mid-1890s the British economy was in recession if not depression adjusting to the new economic order including the growing industrialisation of France and Germany and then the USA. The days of the British success in design and commerce, shown through the building of the Crystal Palace, seemed to be fading. And in London generally, there was also the growth of suburbs where the middle class could strive for the 'new' but in ways which soon became sterile as Dickens portrayed in *Our Mutual Friend* published in 1865:

---

60 Dudley Baines, *Migration in a Mature Economy: Emigration and Internal Migration in England and Wales* (Cambridge: Cambridge University Press, 1985), 279.
61 Ibid., 161–63.
62 Ibid., 182.

> Mr and Mrs Veneering were bran-new people in a bran-new house in a brand new quarter of London. Everything about the Veneerings was spick and span. All their furniture was new, all their friends were new, all their servants were new, their plate was new, their carriage was new, their harness was new, their horses were new, their pictures were new, they themselves were new, they were as newly married as lawfully compatible with their having a bran-new baby, and if they had set up a great grandfather, he would have come home in matting from the Pantechnicon, without a scratch on him, French polished to the crown on his head.[63]

In contrast, the 'new world' of North America, Australia and Argentina, stimulated by new investments in infrastructure such as railways, as well as often speculation in property in the cities, and with rising demand through growing populations, was proving attractive to new migrants as a place for adventure and to make money. And America was a particular 'honey pot' because of its size and possible economic opportunities as well as the prospect of being able to return home fairly quickly if all did not work out. Migration thus became tied to the economic trade cycle across the Atlantic. While Britain was in a 'slump', the 1880s was very prosperous in the USA with cyclical peaks in 1882 and 1887 associated partly with railroad construction.[64]

British emigrants in nineteenth-century America were often regarded as the 'invisible immigrants' – those who soon quickly assimilated into the mainstream of an English-speaking society. A more nuanced view sees different patterns of adaptation according to social and independent circumstances. White-collar middle-class immigrants in the late nineteenth century have been seen to share certain features which marked them out from

---

63 Charles Dickens, *Our Mutual Friend,* opening paragraph to Chapter II entitled 'The Man From Somewhere'.
64 Ibid., 179.

the British emigrants of the early nineteenth century who often came in family groups from rural England. First, they had often left Britain for personal as much as economic reasons. Second, while they had aspirations, and often were white-collar in origin, many brought no special skills or trades. Third, while many European migrants came to America to make money to send back home many of these British white-collar migrants were often seeking further income support from home. Fourth, because they did not come in family groups their sojourn in America was often a lonely one. Tied to no particular community they were often very geographically mobile, pushing forward across the frontiers of settlement.[65]

The migrant experience of members of the extended Sherington family who left for overseas in the 1880s reflects many of these patterns but in very specific and spectacular ways. And migration divided the family in ways that remained unclear to future generations for at least a century.

Murder in America

'Nellie' Sherington and her new husband Steve led the way overseas to America. The upbringing of Nellie suggests that she may have had difficulty in meeting the social expectations of her family particularly after her father died. Sent away at age fourteen to the Ladies College Cambridge House in Leyton in the East End of London, her mother was informed by the headmistress in September, 'You will I trust find her improved. She has certainly given great attention to her studies and has, I believe, taken great

65 Charlotte Erickson, *Invisible Immigrants: The Adaptation of English and Scottish Immigrants in Nineteenth Century America* (London: Cornell University Press, 1972), 393–410.

pains to correct the defects in her character which have been pointed out to her'.[66]

By her mid-twenties Nellie had fallen in love with her future husband Steve, writing passionate love letters to him, but still seeking God's blessing for their union: 'I am glad I love you this evening, because that will keep me good at chapel'. Working in an outfitters' shop in the West End, Steve certainly fitted the image of the urban white-collar Londoner with few skills but high aspirations. And Nellie seems to have been besotted with her lover, soon to be her husband, even though there were some signs that he did not always treat her well. Yet once married he could still write to her as 'My darling Baby' from 'your ever loving hub'.[67] Whereas William Pretty had wooed Annie Sherington through formal and sometimes teasing correspondence the relationship between Nellie and Steve, and even their lives in London, seems to have been a bit 'on the edge' and this became even more true in America.

Nellie and Steve left London in late 1882 or early 1883. They were soon in the Midwest of the United States. In late 1883, Nellie wrote to her sister Annie telling her 'I am safe and well'. Having left England in an apparent hurry Nellie said that it had been better to leave without goodbyes but 'I hope, dear, to send you someday the money I owe your dear husband. I only pray to God to give me health and one day to see you all again'.[68] In a letter written in February 1884 from Kansas City Missouri, Nellie further outlined their new life to her sister Annie. They were now living in a little brick store and 'Steve works late and hard; he is kind again to me, dear, now'. The weather was very cold and

66 Letter, E.J. Walker to 'My dear Mrs Sherrington', 25 September 1867 (courtesy of Mark Shephard).
67 Copies of various correspondence courtesy of Mark Shephard who has provided valuable commentary and insights on the relationship of Nellie and Steve.
68 Letter, Nellie to 'My darling sister Annie', November 1883 (courtesy of Mark Shephard).

there were apparently a number of English migrants there. She liked to read the English newspapers 'but people after they have been here some time don't care for English ways. Many don't even seem interested about the old country – I can't even imagine it myself.' There were material benefits as she had only opened the store for two days and had already taken three dollars. But she was suffering from the cold and thanked Annie for an offer to send her to Florida. There were eight chapels and churches within five minutes' walk including the Wesleyan chapel nearly opposite. And her faith sustained her – 'I am glad, dear, you pray for us, for sometimes I feel very lonely, then I think of a verse or some scriptures and feel better'. And her sister 'Jenny' (Jane?) 'sent me a verse in her letter "I will never forget you nor forsake you" – isn't that sweet'. And then with reference to her health, but also to some past event that may have caused her to depart London:

> I may turn out like the lady you were reading of, and get very strong here. At any rate we must put our confidence in the Lord and hope for the best, and I think dear Annie, one feels really happier than if I had done[?] the wrong. I feel it was not me[?] that brought the trouble and it may, as you told me at home, be sent for a wise purpose, by him who sends rain and sunshine.[69]

The hope in God was still there, perhaps a remnant of the family education under her father and elder sisters, but what was emerging was also faith in the new material prospects of a new land.

Accompanying Nellie and Steve was her younger brother Charlie. In her letter from America in November 1883 Nellie told Annie, 'Charlie is well and in a good situation, if he liked he could do well, but the fault is everyone likes money too fast'. In her May 1884 letter she told her sister: 'Charlie has just come in to see me

69 Letter, Nellie to 'My dearest sister Annie', 6 February 1884 (courtesy of Mark Shephard).

and has been arranging my windows in the store for me. He is a good boy now. I wish he would always be'. Only thirteen years old when his father had died in 1868 Charlie was also thirteen years younger than his older brother William Charles. He seemed to have been closer to his older sisters than to his elder brother. And there were indications of him being strong headed and wilful but also ambitious. In February 1874 William Pretty told Annie that 'Mr Charles came to me a few days ago before leaving for my advice, which from what I know of the young gentlemen, he meant to take, if it coincided with what he intended'. William had advised him to do as William's own brother, Edward Pretty, was doing, 'namely get two or three situations in the leading establishments and see the various methods of conducting business in them, which in my humble opinion would be of immense service to him some day, he himself regretting that he had not taken the same advice even though he had five years behind the counter'. But even as he spoke to him William Pretty could see that Charlie had had enough of retail. Two nights later Charlie told William his sisters wished him to get into wholesale because it was more 'respectable' even though the average 'screw' of a 30-year-old in the wholesale business was under one hundred pounds.[70] And whatever his career in wholesale in London may have been, by 1883 the now twenty-eight-year-old Charlie had joined his sister Nellie and her husband Steve in America.

Nellie and Steve soon moved from the Midwest to California settling in Lake County near San Francisco. In February 1891 the *Examiner* in San Francisco published an article on 'The Riches' as Steve and Nellie had become known (a name perhaps assumed in hope and expectation of wealth). They had apparently lived in Lake County since 1887, Steve previously being secretary of an Australian Improvement Association (possibly an organisation that had arisen out of the trade across the Pacific and move-

70 Letter, William Pretty to Annie Sherington, 8 March 1874 (courtesy of Mark Shephard).

ment of people attracted by the gold fields in both Australia and California). The article pointed out that Steve's real name was Thompson but that being 'financially embarrassed' he had come to the USA under the name of Riche. In Lake County he had followed 'a peaceful law-abiding life'.[71]

According to a letter he wrote to William Pretty in 1891 William Charles Sherington had also arrived in the Lake County area sometime in 1887–88.[72] It seems probable that he had followed or was joining Steve and Nellie. By 1890, William Charles Sherington was working in the mines in Northern California. His sister Nellie and brother-in-law Steve ran a nearby 'small roadside saloon' known as the 'Campers' Retreat' near the Bradford Quicksilver Mine and just outside the centre of Middletown. A family tragedy soon took place.

On the autumn night of 10 October 1890, a group of miners, wearing white caps over their heads, burst into the saloon with the apparent intention of assaulting the 'bouncer' known as Bennett. Effectively this was a vigilante gang disguised in ways similar to other gangs that were then had operating in the Midwest and providing examples that would be later followed by such groups as the Klu Klux Klan. In the melee that followed the invasion, Nellie apparently intervened to protect Steve; she was then shot six times, dying in agony four days later from her wounds. The funeral of Nellie was 'one of the largest ever witnessed in Middletown' with fifty-five vehicles accompanying the hearse to the Methodist Church. The later 'solemn march to the cemetery was followed by the whole community'.[73]

Weeks later Steve also died. William Charles was devastated by these events particularly when he knew some of those ac-

---

71 Helen Rocca Goss, *The California White Cap Murders* (Santa Barbara: Helen Rocca Goss, 1969).
72 Letter, William Charles Sherington to William Pretty, 31 January 1891 (letter is a gift from Mark Shephard, now in Sherington Family Papers).
73 Rocca Goss, *The California White Cap Murders*, 9–15.

cused, and had even been with them just prior to the incident. On 31 January 1891, William wrote home to William Pretty:

> It is about one month since I buried Steve by Nell's side. I can't tell you what I have gone through since that time. He never ought to have made Nell a saloon keeper's wife, but they sought gold and got lead. Since I have been in this country (3 yrs), I have worked on their ranch 18 mo's and had $1 & yet the day of Steve's death he wrote to Charlie and Mother, telling them how bad I was. I nursed Nell 4 days after she was shot and told Steve to get rid of that man Bennett dozens of times. Steve had received a threatening letter telling him to the same thing (of course I did not know this until I went through Steve's papers). After Nell's death, Steve was cross with me because I would not give him my last $20, which I wanted for food, as I have been living all the winter taking charge of the Bullion Mine, living alone amongst the hills. I have joined the Methodist Church and am and have been now abstaining since Nell's death. I cannot draw my money from the Bullion Mine until the end of March as it is bonded. I have had Steve embalmed, so that if Mother wishes them both home it can be done but "In death they were not divided". They lived only for each other and it is a pity to disturb their rest R.I.P. The men who murdered Nell were employed at the Bradford Mine just here and I fancy some of the younger members of that family were conscious of the organized mob. I have had to go to Lakeport twice this month about the will & trial. It is about 38 miles from here – no railroad – and the County seat. This has taken nearly all my cash. Bradfords have opposed me in court each time. They are very rich having gone bail to the amount of 10,000 $ for one man, 5,000 $ each for four others, and three men . . . no bail. Bradfords opposed me with three lawyers, but I won the day and Mr Andrew Rocca (an opposition mine owner and very wealthy) appointed administrator. I am determined that some of these villains shall swing– the trial takes place Feby 2nd. I

> don't think that I shall have to go until Thursday next; if I had spare cash I would go tomorrow. Steve had only about $29 cash when he died and his place is worth about 2500 $. Nell's jewels etc are all safe. Steve left all he had to Nell, which according to the American law goes half to Mother and other half equally divided between her brothers and sisters, but I don't expect after costs there will be much left. I saw Mr Rocca this morning and he would like from Mother a power of attorney to prosecute in this case. It was Steve's wish that if anything happened to him (such as being shot) Mr Rocca should prosecute. We have engaged Clay Taylor a lawyer, a lawyer who prosecutes all the stage robbers in this State, the state going equal shares. If you had nursed Nell as I did, you must excuse this rambling letter, as I feel so full of thoughtful grief and would not have troubled you in the matter, but felt it my duty, being determined to do for them after death what I have done for them when alive i.e. my best.[74]

This was a letter from a tortured man, trying to justify his actions and defend his own role. His appeal for funds stands out but even the disposal of the estate of Nellie and Steve yielded very little.[75]

The personal agony of William Charles was far from over. The trial led to convictions but no hangings for murder. When subsequent efforts were made to either free the men or reduce their sentences by appeal to the Governor, the matter became even more urgent as such efforts involved attacks upon the moral character of his sister and brother-in-law. In February 1892 William Charles wrote from 'Camper's Retreat' to the Governor of California reminding him of his promise to consider what William Charles regarded as the unprovoked murder of his sister. The chief organiser of the raid, 'Blackburn', and his 'gang' were

---

74 Letter, William Charles Sherington to William Pretty, 31 January 1891(courtesy of Mark Shephard).
75 Rocca Goss, *The California White Cap Murders*, 24–25.

responsible for 'three deaths in my family, including my mother', who he said, had died from grief and shock over Nellie's death. He also informed the Governor he had taken notes during the six weeks' trial, and would be glad to forward plenty of details.[76]

Many in the Lake County community supported William Charles. These included the wealthy mine owner Andrew Rocca – mentioned in his letter to William Pretty. But as William Charles had pointed out to William Pretty even before the trial, those charged with murder had influential friends. And the wife of the 'chief organiser' Blackburn had already told the Governor that he should pay no attention to what William Charles said, since 'the poor man is a wreck from drink'.[77] Eventually, those convicted were either pardoned or their sentences commuted or reduced so that none served more than five years.

When the leader of the gang was pardoned, Clay Taylor, the prominent California lawyer and citizen, and the prosecutor at the original trial, wrote to the San Francisco *Examiner* expressing his outrage:

> Under the heading of 'Misplaced Mercy' I note your reference to the commutation of the sentence of Blackburn, one of the Lake County White Caps. Having prosecuted these, and knowing whereof I speak, I want to say that the murder of Mrs Helen Riche by eleven Whitecaps at the 'Campers' Retreat' was, without exception the most atrocious, cowardly and unprovoked murder I have ever investigated during a practice of over twenty years.
>
> It is erroneous to state the crime was committed because the house was conducted there by Riche and his wife was not approved of. The trouble arose from a chastisement which Blackburn received at the hands of one Bennett, who was an

76 Ibid., 68.
77 Ibid., 190.

> employee of the Riches, and it was over a mining claim of Bennett's.
>
> Blackburn organised eleven men into a company and went to the Campers' Retreat in the night time, with the intention of whipping Bennett, who lived at Riche's, with a cat-of-nine tails, tarring and feathering and running him out of the country. All were masked and armed, and upon entering the house Mrs Riche flew to her husband, carrying him his gun, and while so doing she was seized, thrown to the floor and held by one ruffian McGuire, while another fired six bullets into her. Blackburn remained on the front porch, pistol in hand, and probably fired one or more shots into the house. He was the chief and leader of the gang. After the shooting McGuire was found dead on the front porch, a bullet having passed through his body, fired by one of his own crowd, as the proof showed that no shot was fired by anyone else. Mrs Riche lingered four days and died in the greatest agony, and Riche some three months later.
>
> Not a stain or blemish was shown in any of the evidence upon the character of Mrs Riche, who was a pure and beautiful woman, a faithful and loving wife, who gave up her life in defence of her husband and self.[78]

This was at least a fitting memorial to Nellie. The memory of the murder, trial and appeals lingered on in Lake County for over a generation still dividing many in the community, some of whom apparently believed that justice had been done in releasing those who were simply acting to rid the county of undesirables.[79] And even in the 1960s, according to a former colleague at the University of Sydney, who visited Lake County on holidays in his youth, the memory of the murder and the surrounding events

78 Rocca Goss, *The California White Cap Murders*, 71–72.
79 Ibid., 85–108.

lingered on although the invasion of the Camper's Retreat was now seen more like a halloween trick that had gone wrong.[80]

There was a further personal postscript to the murder and trial. In 1933, Chris Yates, a grandson of William and Annie Pretty, visited Lake County and saw the Camper's Retreat building still standing complete with bullet holes. Accompanying him was a University of Cambridge friend named Tom Browning whose American grandfather was a Mr Beakbene living near San Francisco. The two young men spoke to locals who recounted events surrounding the murder of Nellie. Tom then told his parents that Mr Beakbene remembered that he 'actually had another Sherrington (brother of Nellie) in his employment for a few months after her death. He was terribly hard up and Mr B. doesn't know what happened to him afterwards, or his Christian name. He says he was a nice quiet man.'[81]

William Charles Sherington apparently died in San Francisco on 18 March 1897, most likely a broken man. At least his family in Australia, who knew him not, nor even his fate, can now remember him.

What, then, happened to Charlie Sherington? As with his brother, sister and brother-in-law he was one of those many British emigrants who came to America in the 1880s. Unlike his sister and brother-in-law, Charlie Sherington did not leave the Midwest. Instead, he settled for a period in Chicago where there seemed to be many opportunities. He was in Chicago for the World Exhibition of the 1890s – a time of excitement, new buildings and opportunities to make money. In 1892 Charlie told his sister Janey he was running a business and making 'a good living' but that his costs were heavy and so he could not put much away, hence he needed more help from home.[82] And, whilst in

80 Information from Dr Stephen Juan (former lecturer in the Faculty of Education and Social Work, University of Sydney).

81 Letter, Chris Yates to 'Mom and Pop', 14 July 1933 (courtesy of Mark Shephard).

Chicago in 1893, William Pretty asked his wife Annie to send him Charlie's address by 'return to New York and I will leave the two suits when I get there' suggesting that his young brother-in-law may then have been moving between Chicago and New York.[83]

Charlie continued to correspond with his family in London during the early to mid-1890s. With the death of his mother (on receiving news of the murder in Lake County) he continued to press his older siblings to settle the estate, indicating that his circumstances in America were not secure. Obviously distressed by the death of Nellie and then his mother he addressed most of his letters to his sister Jane.[84] The eldest of the children of Charles and Mary Sherington, Mary Jane Sherington, at the age of forty-two, had now married George Charter, Wesleyan Minister, a widower aged forty-nine and also a resident of Upper Norwood. Living at 'Argyle Lodge' on Gipsy Hill, their world of religion and married respectability must have seemed so far away from the bustling 'booster' life of Charlie in late-nineteenth-century Chicago. But while Charlie remains attached at afar to his elder sister, he wanted to maintain his distance from William Charles both geographically and in terms of any future relationships. Once becoming aware of the family tragedy he showed scorn for William's inability to keep the surviving family finances in order, commenting in 1891 on the prospective sale of Nellie and Steve's property – 'I don't know what William is doing. He has got it all his own way. He must have had money off the place for fruit, harvest and lumber'. Concerned for his own financial interests as well as supposedly those of his family, Charlie also felt at first that he should go to California and see what William is doing, plus retrieving Nellie's trinkets and seeing the graves, but

82 Letter, Charlie Sherington to Jane Sherington, 1 December 1892 (courtesy of Mark Shephard).
83 Letter, William Pretty to Anne Pretty, 6 June 1893 (courtesy of Mark Shephard).
84 Various correspondence (courtesy of Mark Shephard).

he appears to be critical of William's habits and behaviour there which were likely to cause scandal – 'I guess William has carried on scandalous down in Middletown'. There was even some disdain for the former Ada Banfield – 'When did you hear from Ada Sherrington. I guess that they have passed from us for ever – small loss to me'. Then he became more antagonistic, 'I should hate to see the sight of William in Chicago. It would make it bad for me'. Nevertheless he tells his sister in March 1892 that he will send on correspondence to William since 'I hope never to forget that he is still my brother & part of my flesh & I shall always treat him all right as far as my human power is concerned'. But two months later, when he learnt from William that nothing was left from Nell's estate, he was more concerned with the legacy he might have received from family properties now that his mother had died, even promising to come home, and requesting that Annie send him his 'quarterly allowance'. He also wrote, 'I pray William will not come to me to bother me in any way. Thank God I have got all I want and that is saying a great deal'. (Charlie even began to see Rocca, the supporter of William in Middletown, as a 'bad man' who had got everything out of the estate of Steve and Nellie.) By August 1892, Charlie had told Janey that he has not heard from William for three months but that a man from Middletown has called on him in Chicago. This man claimed that he had stayed with William for two weeks and that 'William seemed sometimes out of his head, telling the same tales over and over again, then get quite overcome and collapse'. For Charlie this information on William, and the account of the Campers' Retreat and his memories of Nellie and Steve, were too much. He gave up all thought of going to California. Charlie now told Janey he was thinking of buying a small house in Chicago – apparently financed by Janey who would receive the rent. Alternatively, following the death of his mother, he was looking for income from his share of the family estates in Upper Norwood and Holbeach

Lincolnshire.[85] A final letter from Charlie to 'Jeannie' in June 1896 indicates that William had written and was wanting to come to Chicago as he was only earning about three dollars a month– 'that is very small. He sent me his photo, he looks not nice, poor fellow'.[86] William would be dead within a year.

After 1896 there are no surviving letters from Charlie. And his family in England apparently lost contact with him. Does this mean that Charlie finally became one of the British truly 'invisible immigrants'? Perhaps. Perhaps not. One clue may lie in the 1910 US census which reveals the following entry:

> **Charles Skevington** [perhaps Charles Sherington]
> Estimated Age in 1910: 45
> Birthplace: England
> Relation to Head of House: Roomer
> Father's Birth Place: England
> Mother's Birth Place: England
> Home in 1910: Naugatwuck Ward, 1, New Haven,
>   New Connecticut
> Marital Status: Single
> Race: White
> Gender: Male
> Year of Immigration: 1889

On the surface, the name, age and year of immigration do not seem to accord with our Charlie Sherington. But this seems to be the only person in the 1910 US census with a name associated with Charles Sherington. And name changes and pseudonyms were often common practice in this period for various reasons. For instance, Charlie would know that there was an example in his own family with Steve Thompson having changed his name

85 Ibid.

86 Letter, Charlie Sherington to Jane Sherington, various correspondence 1892–96 (courtesy of Mark Shephard).

to Riche. And the memory of his sister's murder and his brother's later 'fuss' in the Midland County might have spurred him further on to change his name. As to age, it is interesting to note that his 'estimated age' is recorded here as being exactly ten years younger than our Charlie Sherington. Any man seeking work in pre-1914 immigrant America would do well to misrepresent his age – to be in your mid-forties was a better prospect for employment than being in your mid-fifties. The date of arrival is also slightly later than we know Charlie came but that may be lack of memory or again effort to conceal age. Overall, being a 'roomer' or lodger in a boarding house was not what Charlie had come to America for. There may be therefore also good reasons why he wished to conceal identity and cut off contacts with his family.

So what can we conclude from all of this? If William Pretty was a late-nineteenth-century entrepreneur with a growing international reputation for success, then the Sheringtons in America were essentially adventurers trusting in luck to restore family fortunes. As William Charles said of Steve and Nellie 'they came for gold' but luck turned against them and they 'got lead'.

For these British migrants from London, the popular image of nineteenth-century America had been associated with the perceived opportunities of an expanding frontier. But there was also another side to the dream of America. In the 1840s, Charles Dickens had journeyed to the United States where he was then known and admired. After travelling along the East Coast, as well as the South and the Midwest, Dickens later published his *Notes* on his visit. The *Notes* held out certain warnings. Not only was America built partly on slavery, but through the knife and gun: 'With sharp points and edges . . . Liberty doth hew and hack her slaves; or, failing that pursuit, her sons devote them to a better use, and turn them on each other'.[87] This was a precisian view of a

87 Charles Dickens, *American Notes and Pictures from Italy* (London: Macmillan and Co., 1893), 211. See also Tomalin, *Charles Dickens: A Life*, 127–42.

culture that would help lead America into civil war in the 1860s. And it was this same culture of violence that would later lead a male vigilante mob to murder Nellie.

Bound for Australia

California, where Nellie, Steve and William Henry Sherington, were buried, was in part tied to Australia through the great gold discoveries of the mid- to late nineteenth century. The historian Eric Hobsbawm has argued that the almost simultaneous discovery of gold in California and Australia in the late 1840s created the new wealth for a 'global industrial economy' and even the beginning of a 'single world history'.[88]

In the wake of the gold rushes in Victoria and New South Wales in the 1850s and 1850s a new economy was built in Australia through what has been seen as a form of 'colonial socialism'. Governments embarked on a program of building ports and railways as well as assisting and subsidising the inflow of migrants.[89] Disenchanted with America, Charles Dickens became a great supporter of migration to Australia, publishing accounts of the migration experience through his edited journal *Household Worlds*, even encouraging two of his sons to migrate.[90] By the 1880s, the idea of settlement in the Empire had become a major counter to those who had simply moved across the Atlantic to the United States.

In contrast to the British who migrated to America, many British migrants to Australia were on government-assisted pas-

---

88 Eric Hobsbawm, *The Age of Capital, 1848–1875* (London: Abacus, 2003), 63.
89 N.G. Butlin, A. Barnard and J.J. Pincus, *Government and Capitalism* (Sydney: George Allen and Unwin, 1982), 13–18.
90 Margaret Mendelawitz (ed.), *Charles Dickens' Australia: Selected Essays from Household Word, 1850–1859, Book Two: Immigration* (Sydney: Sydney University Press, 2011). See also Tomalin, *Charles Dickens: A Life*, 337, 371–73.

sages. The length of the voyage to the Antipodes meant that they knew when they embarked that they would remain in Australia for a long time – perhaps forever. In Australia, there was no view of an expanding frontier, as there was in America, except perhaps for the open spaces of northern Australia. The vast majority of late-nineteenth-century immigrants to Australia remained in the cities or towns along the coast comforted by the view that even if the climate was different there were still elements of a common British or even English culture tied to 'home'.[91]

It was this move to be part of the Empire of settlement that probably lay behind the decision of Ada Sherington and her sisters to rebuild the family fortunes by leaving England and heading south to Queensland. This was to be an emigration of the three Banfield sisters: Ada with her three sons, but also the unmarried Clara and Alice. The relevant street directories and newspaper advertisements indicate that it was about 1888 that Clara gave up the glass and crystal business at Silverdale Terrace, Sydenham. If there was sale or proceeds from the business this may have been not to repay debts, as Olive Sherington suggested in 1970, but to help fund the voyage to Australia. Henry Banfield, now in his sixties, remained in England but was not attached any longer to a crystal and glass business. He probably moved to Sussex not long after his daughters left for Australia. He died in around 1896.

The issue of available family finances may also explain why all three sisters decided to emigrate to Australia under assisted passage schemes and particularly why they chose to go to Queensland. During the 1880s Queensland was the colony most actively recruiting new settlers, many of whom came to not only Brisbane but also to the coastal centres such as Townsville, Rockhampton and Maryborough. To compete with migration to North America, the Australian colonies had long offered assisted

---

91 James Jupp, *The English in Australia* (Melbourne: Cambridge University Press, 2004), 110–17.

passages. The height of assisted immigration to Queensland was in 1882 when over 28 000 men, women and children arrived, but there was a continuous flow of people until the Depression of the early 1890s.[92] Principally because of immigration the overall Queensland population expanded by eighty per cent in the 1880s with the growth in Brisbane being more than double that rate.[93] Queensland in the 1880s seemed to be the 'boom' colony of Australia.

And then there was the issue of social class. During the nineteenth century much of the assisted migration to Australia was working class in origin, with the colonial government mainly helping families, single men and female domestic servants. But from the mid-1860s a number of middle-class emigration societies in Britain had concentrated on the fate of the 'redundant woman' who had been unable to find a husband or gain employment in Britain. These promoters of middle-class female emigration urged the Australian colonial governments to allow middle-class women to receive assisted or even free passage to Australia. Thomas Archer, Queensland agent general in London during the 1880s, was sympathetic to providing free or assisted passages to the 'better type' of Englishwoman.[94]

Migration was now much quicker and more comfortable. From the early 1880s the British Steam Navigation Company operated ships from London to Australia. There were matrons on board and supervision of passenger conditions. This all supported the migrant ships leaving for Queensland.[95] The two Banfield sisters, and then Ada – under the name of Sherington – left London in a staged and perhaps deliberately strategic fashion. On 18 July 1888, Alice Banfield, 'nurse', aged twenty-four, departed

---

92 Jan Gothard, *Blue China: Single Female Migration to Colonial Australia* (Melbourne: Melbourne University Press, 2001), 230–31.
93 Geoffrey Sherington, *Australia's Immigrants,1788–1988* (Sydney: Allen and Unwin), 83.
94 Gothard, *Blue China*, 59–62.
95 Jupp, *The English in Australia*, 114.

Plymouth on the *Famenoth* a small ship of 899 tons, bound for Maryborough. Alice had an assisted passage along with thirty-three others, mainly males but the vast majority of passengers, 171 in total, were those bound for domestic service or general labourers. They were drawn from across Britain and Ireland but few seemed to have come from London. On 2 November 1888, after a voyage of three and a half months, the ship arrived at Maryborough where Alice supposedly disembarked. She had arrived in Australia towards the end of the year celebrating the centenary of British settlement in Australia but she was probably not aware of the significance of this.[96]

On 18 September 1888, Clara Banfield, received a free passage as a 'domestic' on the much larger 2545-ton *Dacca* which finally arrived in Brisbane on 12 November 1888, after a voyage of less than two months, and having dropped off immigrants at the various ports along the Queensland coast. The *Dacca* had carried 532 passengers, of whom 158, mainly women such as Clara, had travelled as future domestics, as well as 252 known as 'remittance' immigrants who had been nominated by someone in Queensland who had agreed to pay the passage and with the prospect that the nominee would support them once they arrived in the colony. At age thirty, Clara was one of the oldest women on board.[97]

Ada Sherington, now aged thirty-eight, and her three sons William, fourteen, Arthur, twelve, and Guy, ten, left London on 3 April 1889 on the *Taroba* of 3235 tons. In an obvious attempt to qualify for the passage assistance scheme, designed principally either for single persons or married couples and their children, Ada described her status as 'widow', aged 34. Ada and her three boys were 'remittance' immigrants, along with 145 others of the total of 545 passengers, but it is not clear who had nominated

96 Passenger Lists, Queensland State Archives, Item ID 18487.
97 Ibid., Item ID 18485.

them and paid for their passage unless it was either Alice or Clara Banfield who had already arrived in Queensland.

Ada and Arthur wrote home to family and friends in Upper Norwood from Port Said and in return William received some correspondence when he arrived in Brisbane. There was also a school on board the ship educating twenty-six boys and twenty-one girls aged under twelve. According to Olive Sherington's correspondence to Richard Sherington in 1970, during the voyage 'a committee of four women was formed to aid the captain in keeping up the cleanliness of the ship . . . [Ada] used to laugh when she recalled that the only illness on the ship was Arthur's case of measles, which was isolated in the bathroom'. After about six weeks the *Taroba* arrived in Brisbane on 24 May 1889 (the birthday of Queen Victoria, later known as Empire Day).[98]

In contrast to the Sheringtons in America, the Banfield–Sherington journey to Australia was a more traditional form of assisted migration destined to end up in urban Australia. Despite the image of the 'distressed gentlewoman' it was still unusual for females, such as Ada Sherington, to head middle-class families (perhaps less so in the working-class family where deaths of the male breadwinner could leave widows as the formal head of the household). It was even rarer for the female head of such a family to migrate along with her sisters and children. The new Banfield–Sherington alliance of three sisters and three young brothers would face re-building family fortunes in the new environment of the Antipodes. There was family work to be done within the context of the British Empire of settlement rather than an America of disappointed opportunity. It would soon be seen whether this strategy would succeed.

98 Passenger Lists, Queensland State Archives, Item ID18485.

Charles Sherington, c.1850.

Social housing on Central Hill, Upper Norwood, 2013 – the former site of the Sherington home 'Codrington Villa'.

Mark Shephard in 2010 in front of 5 Gipsy Hill, once a Sherington home now a dental surgery.

Upper Norwood was part of the suburban expansion of London.

Views of the Crystal Palace in 1860.

Mark Shephard in 2010 at the former Crystal Palace site.

The Pretty factory at Ipswich.

Clara Banfield's chinaware business address at 2 Silverdale Terrace at Lower Sydenham, down the hill from Crystal Palace.

William Pretty.

Annie Pretty (nee Sherington).

The family home of Henry Banfield in 1870, 3–4 Palace Grove, Penge, near Crystal Palace.

Helen Sherington, also known as Nellie, c.1880.

Middletown cemetery California. Opened in 1889, it was the last resting place of Helen Sherington who died in 1890.

The family home of William Charles and Ada Caroline Sherington in the 1870s, at 1 Bermuda Villas (now 61 Underhill Road) near Upper Norwood.

From the left: the three brothers Arthur, William and Guy Sherington, c.1887.

Chemist shop on Westow Hill, Upper Norwood where William Henry Sherington worked in the 1880s, still standing when his son and grandson visited the site in 1973.

In the middle: William Pretty at his family home 'Goldrood', Ipswich, c.1913. On the left are his sons William and Ernest and on the right are his sons Frank and Donald.

III
Sydney: The Globite Story

> Men do not emigrate in despair, but in hope . . . There is very little room in the old country but plenty of room in the colonies and the men who come to Australia in search of room; they expect a larger return on their capital and a higher price for their labour; they leave a land where opportunities seem to be shrinking to a land where the expanding chances may lead them anywhere.
>
> W.K. Hancock, *Australia* (London: Ernest Benn, 1930), 54.

Family Ties Across the Globe

The Sheringtons who left for America arrived there in the 1880s – a decade of prosperity. In the end the hope of quick wealth through gold had led to only disappointment and death. The Banfield–Sherington family union had arrived in Australia after three decades of the long post–gold rushes boom when colonial governments had borrowed in Britain to build the infrastructure to encourage economic growth. The land boomed, financed often by British banks. This was all part of 'colonial socialism'.[1] The 1890s in Australia would be a difficult decade of economic depression. At the beginning of the 1890s banks crashed. This marked the end of economic development in Australian cities during the previous decades. There was soon industrial unrest and great strikes across rural Australia and on the wharves. But amidst all this upheaval the 1890s can also be seen as an era of cultural and social change, where people looked forward to the turn of the century and the prospect of a new federated nation.[2] Some newcomers could foresee new ways forward. Government support for immigration collapsed and numbers arriving declined in the 1890s but the support of family within Britain and Australia often sustained new arrivals. There were also issues here of gender boundaries. Historians now draw attention to single female middle-class migrants in such occupations as governesses and teaching.[3] But the Banfield–Sherington family was led by women with an eye for a new enterprise that would restore fortunes and provide a living for the young males as 'independent Australian Britons'. It was this expectation that would shape Sherington family strategies for the first decade in Australia.

There was also some hope for the future. The Australian economy was changing in the late nineteenth century even with the onset of the 1890s depression. Manufacturing's share of gross domestic product had already grown from 5.3 per cent in the gold rush period of the 1850–60s to 11.8 per cent in 1891; the number of factories in New South Wales and Victoria expanded from

1 Noel George Butlin et al., *Government and Capitalism* (Sydney: Allen and Unwin, 1982), 13–18.
2 Melissa Bellanta, 'Rethinking the 1890s' in Stuart Macintyre and Alison Bashford (eds), *The Cambridge History of Australia*, vol. 1 (Melbourne: Cambridge University Press, 2013), 218–41.
3 Gothard, *Blue China*, 203–08.

1132 at mid-century to 6197 in 1891. With the recovery in the late 1890s there seemed to be some future in owning a factory.[4]

Hope also lay in the economic merging of the separate colonies. Federation in 1901 brought not only a sense of national identity but a national market for goods which were soon protected from foreign imports by a national tariff. More generally, Australia's economy was slowly being transformed from dependence on agriculture to increasing reliance on manufacturing.

In the first decade of the twentieth century Australian manufacturing would outstrip agriculture. Economic recovery in individual states was complete by 1905 and there was a new boom by 1913. Migration revived even bringing in skilled workers. New industries grew up around the utilisation of rural products such as leather and textiles. State investment led to the opening of new lines of communication and specifically the new rail and transport infrastructure in cities and country. Passenger traffic expanded as much as the transport of material goods. All this supported the new area of commercial and consumer travel associated with 'travel goods' – the very area the Sheringtons were about to invest in.[5]

Ada Caroline Sherington, her three sons and two sisters were actually well placed to take advantage of these impending changes in Australia. These middle-class immigrants had aspirations and some cultural and material capital as well as commercial if not manufacturing skills. Ada at least had a background in her own family's experience in retail. Her sons were on the verge of adulthood and William at least carried references from his employer in London.

Initially, they stayed in Brisbane, their port of arrival. For two years William Henry was employed by Finney Isles and

---

4 Peter Cochrane, *Industrialisation and Dependence: Australia's Road to Economic Development, 1870–1939* (St Lucia: University of Queensland Press, 1980), 1.

5 Butlin et al., *Government and Captitalism*, 18–28.

Co., merchants located in the City Exchange on the corner of Queen Adelaide and Edward Streets. He worked in haberdashery and the department concerned with country orders.[6] Brisbane was growing in the late nineteenth century, but its population at 86 000 in 1888 was still only about one quarter of Sydney at 358 000.[7] The capital of Queensland was in many ways still a large country town – a metropolitan centre of government buildings with extended suburbs. Larrikin gangs inhabited Brisbane's 'frog hollow', terrorising women and the Chinese.[8] In contrast, Sydney had its larrikin gangs but was also challenging Melbourne as the major capital city of Australia. In the 1890s the population of Sydney grew by over 100 000 so that by the time of Federation, Sydney, the founding city of British settlement in 1788, had overtaken the population of 'Marvellous Melbourne', the city of wealth from the gold rushes. Sydney certainly provided far more opportunities than Brisbane for those seeking to re-establish their fortunes. Increasingly it was a place for entrepreneurs and enterprise.

The Sheringtons and Banfield sisters soon moved from Brisbane to Sydney. In May 1892 the Sherington family home was at 2 Cheapside Woolloomooloo, just near the docks of Sydney. Success for them now depended much on the contacts of extended family. William Henry had already written to his uncle William Pretty for advice and support. William Pretty soon replied that he had asked a friend of his in Sydney, a 'Mr Smith', to arrange with his agent Wilkins, who had been in Sydney for some time, to recommend some lodgings. There was also the prospect of some venture capital.

The new settlers could rely on their connections in London and Suffolk. Despite the divorce the Banfields remained on good,

---

6 Sherington Family Papers.

7 Graeme Davison et al., *Australians 1888* (Sydney: Fairfax Syme & Weldon, 1988), 189.

8 Bellanta, 'Rethinking the 1890s', 224.

even warm terms, with both the extended Sherington family and the Prettys. Mary Sherington, wife of Charles who had died in 1868, took a great interest in her three Sherington grandsons. In May 1889, as Ada and her sons approached Australia, she told her granddaughter Hilda, the child of Annie and William Pretty, 'I have written to Arthur today he will see his new home in a week or so. I hope they will like Brisbane. I am told it is very hot'.[9]

William Pretty provided more material support. He had instructed a 'Mr Chapman' to hand over the 'rest of the money' that he had sent for Ada Caroline with the 'hope it will be of some service to her. I shall not require any re-payment'. He also agreed with their move from Brisbane urging William to stay with the draper's Farmers and Company, adding 'it is a good firm, and I don't believe in frequent changes'. On a more personal note he indicated that he had sent on Guy's letters to Frank Pretty who was then at school in Eastbourne.[10]

The Pretty family connection would remain vital for the early success of the Sheringtons in Australia. Not only was it a continuation of past family associations, it would become a major support for new opportunities. But new family associations in Sydney would also provide the basis for these opportunities. By 1895, William Henry had decided to leave Farmers' and enter the business of Alfred Ford, the future husband of William's aunt Clara Banfield. Born in Bethnal Green London c.1849, the son of a customs officer, Alfred Ford had first been married in Plymouth England to Sarah Ann Chown in 1870. They had one daughter. In the early 1880s Ford had migrated to Australia. He had started his business in about 1887 as a manufacturer of metal trunks and an importer of china and glass. Ford had apparently run into economic difficulties, perhaps because of the depres-

9 Letter, Mary Sherington to 'My Very dear Hilda', 16 May 1889 (letter gift of Mark Shephard).

10 Letter, W. Pretty to W. Sherrington [sic.], 27 June 1892 (Sherington Family Papers).

sion of the early 1890s. As a result, the business of Alfred Ford was now in the hands of accountants who were acting for creditors. Although reassured by the creditors' accountants that it was a sound business, Ada Caroline Sherington sought advice from William Pretty and his agent in Sydney as to whether she should put in some money into the business which was formerly at Newton and Oxford Street but now located at Ultimo. This would be on the basis that the firm would provide for William – William apparently got on well with Ford, and Ford was looking for a partner. Ford had apparently informed Ada Caroline that if she could get £150 together he would take her son William Henry. Ada now intended to raise part of the money through insurance policies and William Henry had raised the question whether William Pretty could provide surety. There was also an accountant named Joseph Moses who had managed Ada Caroline's father's business in London; he was apparently returning to Sydney at the end of the year and knew something of Ford's business. She herself thought the business a 'good one', the machinery was 'very expensive' and was the only 'good factory' of the kind 'capable of great extension'. But again she looked to William Pretty and his agent for guidance on whether the Ford business was worthwhile.[11]

In Sydney Ada Caroline depended on the support of her eldest son William Henry. More than thirty years later, at Christmas 1923, she presented William, now married and with a large family, with a gold locket containing his portrait as a child. There was a small note inside with the inscription 'To my eldest son with prayers which he and his dear one's may have every blessing and in memory of the hard times (he and I) had when we first started our home'.[12] It was perhaps a reflection on not just the early period in Australia but the years in South London. Disappoint-

11 Ada Caroline Sherington, undated correspondence c.1895 (Sherington Family Papers).
12 In possession of the authors.

ment in marriage had led to not just hopes and expectations for her sons but a bond with her eldest child.

In late 1895, William Henry Sherington wrote to his uncle William Pretty:

> You will receive a letter from Mother also by the same mail in which she explained more fully the hopes that I have of pushing my way on & bettering myself. At present I am still at Farmers where I have been since I came to Sydney 3 1/2 years ago I am very thoughtful that the business is conducted in a very strict manner and the lessons I have learnt will serve me in after life but it is not a house in which you can have any hope of securing a good position & it rather spoils any ambition you may have when you see the hands are either so poorly paid or are retired . . . Mr Ford who is engaged to my aunt upon hearing that I was dissatisfied suggested that I should join him in his line which I think is Tin Trunk manufacturing & other small things, as Coal shuttles but the main business is the trunks for which he also holds a patent, another improvement he has registered. As far as I can see the business is one that with a little management could be made to succeed handsomely.[13]

In March 1896, William Henry Sherington left Farmer and Company and joined Alfred Ford as his accountant. William Pretty agreed to guarantee the company's bank overdraft of £300. The accountants, acting for the company McLean Bros and Riggs Ford to whom Ford had owed money, were now prepared to release control over the business on the understanding that Alfred Ford paid 30/- per week plus stock.[14] In practice William Henry was now the 'junior' partner to Alfred Ford in the business. And

---

13 Letter, William Henry Sherington to William Pretty, c.September 1895 (Sherington Family Papers).
14 Notes on History of Ford Sherington (Sherington Family Papers).

it some respects it was a real partnership. The latter view of Olive Sherington has some bite but only a substance of very limited truth:

> Clara [Banfield] met and marries a certain Alfred Ford, a vain, and I think, a very stupid little fellow. He had the business of Alfred Ford and sad to say, for Clara's sake, the fortnight after her marriage to him, she found out that he was on the verge of being a bankrupt. It was then the three sons of Ada [Caroline] came into the picture . . . To save their aunt, who had helped in their upbringing in many ways, they took over the firm, which became Ford Sherington Limited. [Ada Caroline] bought the first pieces of machinery in change from the manufacture of tin trunks to suitcases, footballs, handbags etc.[15]

In effect, Ada Caroline knew of Alfred Ford's financial difficulties before he married her sister Clara. And as the above correspondence from Ada Caroline and William Henry to William Pretty reveals, it could be said that Ford was offering William an opportunity. Ford obviously knew the value of patents and the significance of manufacturing and marketing a brand. The surviving first record of his business is a wages book of August 1887 which lists Alfred Ford as 'Tin Trunk Maker'. The following year in *Sands Directory* A. Ford is listed as an 'Ironmonger' at 319 King Street, Newtown. The next year his *Sands Directory* listing also included a warehouse of china and glass at both 64 Oxford Street, Sydney and 319 King Street, Newtown. He had obviously made good in the 1880s but perhaps did not know how to manage the business which now continued for over a decade to be still known as Alfred Ford and Company. His venture into glass and china was a link to the business Clara Banfield had conducted, although Ford soon had other ventures. By 1891 Alfred Ford owned four and a half acres with a considerable value of £300.

15 Letter, Olive Sherington to Richard Sherington, 1970.

Still in his mid-forties perhaps he was not a bad catch for Clara Banfield after all, despite what some of the family saw as his unfortunate personality.

As partners with Alfred Ford, the Sherington family 'lived above the shop' just as William Pretty once did at Ipswich. And every morning they opened the factory in Harris Street Ultimo for the workforce. By 1897 there were fifteen employees. And slowly the business diversified into new products apart from tin trunks.[16]

Part of the early-nineteenth-century estate of surgeon William Harris, Harris Street was built out by the end of the 1880s with terraces and shops. The business of Alfred Ford was located just along from the original Bristol Arms Hotel built on the corner of Harris and Quarry Streets in 1874–75. The Alfred Ford factory was actually between Quarry Street and Willam Henry Street which was named after one of the Harris family. By the 1870s, Ultimo had both large mansions and terrace housing. By the 1880s there were also the small factories which were to become the feature of the area. In particular, Harris Street developed in the 1880s with a mixture of houses, shops and small industrial enterprises. Over time, dozens of different trades and industries occupied sites in the street, with many of the shops and industries providing accommodation for the owners and operators like the Sheringtons.[17]

Ada Caroline soon acquired a reputation as the woman who rescued Alfred Ford, a view that persisted in the Sydney business community well into the next generation.[18] And it was obviously a good business investment. In 1898, she was able to buy land

16 Notes on History of Ford Sherington c.1960; William George Sherington Memoirs c.1977; Interview with William George Sherington, 1977 (Sherington Family Papers).
17 Shirley Fitzgerald and Hilary Golder, *Pyrmont and Ultimo* (Sydney: Hale and Iremonger, 1994), 60–61.
18 William George Sherington Memoirs; Interview with William George Sherington.

in Park Avenue, Manly for £200 with the prospect of probably building near her sister Clara and Alfred Ford. In July 1901 Ada and her sons moved from Ultimo to 'Sandlina' Ocean Street Bondi but she was soon living at 'Bon Accord' in Bon Accord Avenue, Waverley.[19] The social activities of the Sherington brothers were now more centred on the Eastern Suburbs which were expanding particularly on the heights around Bellevue Hill and Bondi looking down on the harbour and the old Cooper and Wentworth Estates which would not be broken up until the eve of the First World War.

The Sheringtons soon became sportsmen. Guy and Arthur were founding members of the Bondi Surf Club in 1907; Guy joined the prestigious White City tennis club. Most important of all was sailing. At the 'Commonwealth Acquatic Demonstration' held on 4 January 1901 to celebrate the new Australian Federation, William's boat *Westra* was second in the last race of the day held for boats 18 feet and under.[20]

The '18 footers' were the boats of spectacle on early-twentieth-century Sydney Harbour, built for speed and show, carrying large crews and lots of sail. As a result there were many spectacular capsizes. William, Arthur and Guy soon had their own eighteen footer for racing, *WAG*, to celebrate their initials as a bit of a 'gag'; the boat even had the future Rugby League international Dally Messenger in the crew.[21]

While the Sheringtons became principally an Eastern Suburbs family in the first decade of Australian Federation, social relations with inner-city families were maintained through St John's Church Glebe on the other side of Darling Harbour which fronted onto Ultimo. Of Romanesque design in Pyrmont sandstone, and designed by Edmund Blacket, the leading architect

---

19 Notes on History of Ford Sherington.
20 Commonwealth Acquatic Demonstration Official Programme, 4 January 1901 (Sherington Family Papers).
21 William George Sherington Memoirs.

in nineteenth-century Sydney, St John's opened in 1870. As with many churches in the late nineteenth century St John's was a centre of sporting teams and other activities such as an institute which held evenings of talk and discussion (St John's was also close to the Glebe estate which provided income to the Sydney Anglican Church). The Sherington brothers all played leading roles in the institute in the 1890s. And it was through St John's Church that the Sheringtons came into contact with the Oxbys from New Zealand who were then living at Glebe Point. The Sherington brothers seem to have met some of the Oxby clan through playing rugby. And eventually this led to romantic attachment between William Henry Sherington and Mabel Helen Oxby.

The background of the Oxbys was English, rural, and immig rant. William Oxby was born in Nottinghamshire in 1839. His wife Emily Saville was born in Essex in 1847. On her mother's side, the family lineage stretched back into the seventeenth century through marriage alliances in Essex in or around the centre of Great Waltham.[22] William and Edith were both part of the mid-nineteenth-century migration to New Zealand often from southern rural England. They married in New Zealand in 1869. They had six children with Sid, born in 1878, and Mabel, born in 1880, being the youngest. While living at Timaru on the east coast of the South Island, William was involved in a sea rescue which would lead to his death. The *Ben Venue* a coal ship from Newcastle New South Wales was wrecked by rough seas off Timaru on 5 May 1882. The crew abandoned ship and sought refuge on the *City of Perth* which then also faced difficulties and was then abandoned also. Lifeboats and also a surfboat crew of volunteers set out from the Timaru harbour. The surf boat was swamped and its crew had to be rescued. Crew from the *City of Perth* and watermen from Timaru drowned. William Oxby was a member of the surf boat crew. He died the next year, suffering

22 Research of Barbara Dawson.

from the effects of that incident.[23] A stone memorial and the surf boat itself still stands in Timaru.

Despite the loss of William Oxby the family seemed to have survived the New Zealand economic depression of the 1880s which led to many settlers leaving for Australia. The Oxby women at least showed some independence in remaining in New Zealand. Emily registered as a 'widow' to vote in the 1893 New Zealand elections, the first occasion in the world in which females could vote. As did her daughter Mary Caroline Oxby who registered as a school teacher. The entire Oxby family of Edith and her children eventually moved to Sydney in the 1890s. By the early twentieth century various directories indicated that the Oxbys were living at Glebe, Woollahra, and around North Sydney, in Mosman.[24] The *Sands Directories* for 1902–03 also indicate that there was a Walker–Oxby partnership as produce merchants in Erskine Street in the city.[25]

Family misfortune and tragedies thus brought the Sheringtons and the Oxbys together. William Henry and Mabel Helen married at St John's Church Glebe in 20 September 1904. William Henry described himself as 'manufacturer' of Bondi; Mabel Helen was a 'spinster' of Glebe Point. They went to live at Bondi and then at Bellevue Hill.

William Henry's Sherington's position was now more assured by the growing profits of the business and the increasing role of the Sherington brothers in the enterprise. In 1901 the youngest brother Guy had joined Alfred Ford. In 1902, William began to negotiate arrangements, backed by his mother, whereby the family would become an equal partner with Alfred Ford. This meant putting in extra capital. As Olive Sherington has suggested, this included, on Ada Sherington's part, the purchase of machinery to

23 Research of Barbara Dawson and notes of William George Sherington.
24 Research of Barbara Dawson.
25 Ibid.

enable the firm to move more into leather goods. In June 1902, his uncle William Pretty informed him that he was 'anxious' to see all his Sherington nephews do well and would thus provide a guarantee with the Sherington family's bankers for £500 on payment of four per cent annually for five years on the expectation that it would be paid off in that period. By October 1902 he had agreed to raise the guarantee to £800 (in 1906 the guarantee was transferred from London Bank of Australia to Bank of Australasia). With capital in the company now at £1,326.13.10, a formal partnership emerged between Ada Caroline and Alfred Ford with her land at Manly being deposited with the bank as security. All three brothers were now in the business with Arthur leaving a printing company and joining Alfred Ford at a salary of three pounds per week.[26]

Within six months of the new agreement the business had moved from Ultimo on the outskirts of the city to a site in almost the centre of the manufacturing heart of the city. The multi-storied premises at 278–280 Elizabeth Street, very close to the planned Central Railway station, was first leased for three years, and then from August 1906, the expanded premises of 274–80 was rented for seven years, at seven pounds per week for a year and then eight pounds per week thereafter. As early as 1900 the business had already begun to produce leather goods as well as tin trunks. The firm of Alfred Ford now expanded from being essentially a large workshop establishment into a real small factory with different production methods. By December 1903, there were already thirty-two employees. The move also allowed the business to shift the nature of its manufacturing production.[27]

William Henry now told his uncle William Pretty that the guarantee his uncle had provided would enable the company to produce 'fashionable' ladies' and men's leatherwear. In reply, William Pretty indicated that he thought the prospects looked good

---

26 Notes on History of Ford Sherington.
27 Notes on History of Ford Sherington.

but he did not consider the business large enough to become a limited company. Rather, as partners they should keep the property in their own hands for some time to come. His son Frank and he had not forgotten to send any 'novelty' they might think useful for them to copy but 'corsets and leather goods are far apart, and we never come across leather goods'. But he was sending the price list of the chief English firm of 'case makers' who made both 'travellers' sample cases' and 'Tin cases'.[28]

For the next five or six years, William Henry wrote constantly to his uncle informing him how the company was going. In return, William Pretty often requested advice on the balance sheet and the profits earned. With growing prosperity in Australia, sales grew rapidly and steadily. In the six months to April 1903 sales had been £2786; in the six months to April 1907 they were £11,206. And complementing the correspondence was personal contact. In 1904, William Pretty's son Ernest visited Sydney and probably visited the factory to see what was being made. In May 1906, Frank Pretty, who had been a boyhood friend of Guy Sherington, called into the factory in Elizabeth Street.[29]

Within this context of growth and expansion, the Sherington brothers were now anxious for further control of the business of Alfred Ford. Ford himself was apparently becoming increasingly just a spectator taking little active part in either the manufacturing or management of the firm he had founded. Following further negotiations in October 1907 a new agreement between Alfred Ford and Ada Sherington was signed for five years. Ford was to receive six pounds per week from the business and Ada Caroline 10/-. Each of the three Sherington brothers would receive a salary of £4.10.0 per week. Profits would be shared in proportions with 2/5 to Alfred Ford, 1/5 to Ada Caroline and 2/5 shared between the three brothers. William Henry was appoin-

28 Letter, William Henry Sherington to 'Mr Pretty', 1 March 1904; Letter, W. Pretty to William, 7 April 1904 (Sherington Family Papers).
29 Sherington Family Papers; Notes on History of Ford Sherington.

ted manager for five years as well as his role as chief accountant and cashier.[30]

This was the first stage of a Sherington 'take over' of the business of Alfred Ford. By 1910, the Sherington brothers were moving towards the establishment of a limited liability company. This may have been prompted by the position of William Pretty. In March, he replied to an earlier correspondence of William Henry regarding the current profits of the company. While agreeing that 'competition we know often interferes with profit' William Pretty believed that on a trade of £21 000 the business ought to be making more than £500 which was only two and a half per cent. He was also concerned about increasing bad debts and the rising overdraft which he wanted to see reduced as 'I am getting old and don't want to leave any responsibilities behind me'.[31]

Whatever the final motivation, it was now agreed to sell the business of Alfred Ford to a new company, Ford Sherington Limited which was now registered under the *Companies Act 1874* (NSW). An agreement dated 13 December 1910 provided for the new company to be responsible principally for the 'manufactures and dealers in travelling requisites' as well as for other products such as 'sheet metal goods sports goods motor accessories fancy leather goods'. Under the agreement the company could also apply for patents and acquire property. The registered capital under the *Companies Act* was 50 000 shares of one pound each but with provision for Alfred Ford and Ada Caroline Sherington to hold preference shares with certain entitlements including approval of any borrowings by the company. Most of the share capital was not issued at the outset and there was also provision for the sale

30 Various correspondence of solicitors and others, c.1907; Notes on History of Ford Sherington.

31 Letter, W. Pretty to William Sherrington [sic.], 17 March 1910 (Sherington Family Papers).

of shares so as to keep ownership essentially in the hand so of the original shareholders.[32]

Under this agreement, Alfred Ford kept his initial primacy in the name of the company, and received considerable financial benefits and returns, while the Sherington family received less financial consideration but were the moving force behind the limited liability company. Ford received 3000 one-pound 'A' preference shares with a fixed dividend of £500 per annum for five years, or on earlier death, £250 per annum of Alfred Ford and wife Clara. On death of both parties, 'A' preference shares would revert to 'B' preference shares with fewer entitlements. Initially Ada Caroline Sherington received 3000 preference shares of one pound each. At the first meeting of the Company in January 1911 she directed that these shares be divided between her two sons, William and Guy, who were now also the two directors of Ford Sherington. William Henry Sherington and John Guy Sherington each received 243 ordinary shares and Arthur Charles (who had now left Alfred Ford) 200 shares all at one pound. In December 1912 Ada Caroline Sherington was issued with a further 600 ordinary shares which she passed on to her sons William and Guy in equal parts. In terms of management Alfred Ford would still chair the meeting of the directors of the new company, and seems to have called himself 'managing director', but the ideas and initiative now and in the future came from the two Sherington brothers.[33]

Ford Sherington Limited

From its inception, Ford Sherington was a family affair. Much in the Sherington family had previously depended on Ada Caroline

32 Memorandum of Articles of Association of Ford Sherington Limited (Sherington Family Papers).

33 Ford Sherington Directors' Meeting Minutes, January 1911 and December 1912; Notes on History of Ford Sherington.

Sherington who had brought her sons to Australia accompanied by her sisters. Essentially she had achieved what she had set out to do – re-build the family fortunes lost in London. Small in stature, she still remained the virtual founder of the new family enterprise in Australia, and all her sons would continue to seek her advice. But she was now in her late fifties and the business had now truly passed from the partnership she had with Alfred Ford into the management hands of her sons. In 1916, she moved from Waverley to Manly to be close to her sister Clara, who was married to Alfred Ford, and her younger sister Alice, long known as 'Nurse Banfield' who had tramped the northern beaches and their districts often late at night delivering babies; Alice's reputation increased as post-1918 soldier settlers and others took up blocks in the hinterland behind the beaches. And Ada Caroline would also entertain her oldest grandson for a day or two at Manly, leaving a strong impression that she believed it was more important to have a family of boys rather than girls.[34]

Of all the three Sherington brothers, Arthur Charles was least committed to the day-to-day management of Ford Sherington. Perhaps, as Olive Sherington has suggested, this was because he recognised the emerging differences between his two brothers that would become more pronounced over the years.[35] More likely he saw an opportunity to make his own mark, leaving Alfred Ford in 1909 to become the agent for William Pretty in Australia. During 1911 he travelled to England to meet the relatives he had not seen since leaving London two decades earlier, including his aunt Jeannie, the sister of Annie Pretty (Alfred and Clara Ford were apparently also in London at the same time).[36] He may even have gone into the sky: a photo has survived showing a rather nervous Arthur in a biplane in England in 1911.[37] In

34 Interview with William George Sherington.
35 Letter, Olive Sherington to Richard Sherington, 1970.
36 Various correspondence in Sherington Family Papers.
37 Photo courtesy of Mark Shephard.

1911, William Henry was still the only married brother. He was also becoming a family man with responsibilities. Mabel Helen and William Henry now had four children – Ada Mabel (born in 1905), William George (born in 1907), Dorothy Emily (born in 1909), and Marjorie Clara (born in 1911). The twins, Charles Alfred and Frank Henry, would be born in 1913 and Donald Saville in 1916. The family had originally lived in the rented premises 'Beauchef' at Bellevue Road, Woollahra where Ada and William were born with 'Nurse Alice Banfield' as the midwife. By the time Dorothy was born, the family had moved to Beecroft, which was then on the outskirts of the North Shore of Sydney. Of slight build, William Henry was probably concerned for his health and this may have prompted the move to the 'healthy air' of the northern suburbs of Sydney. The family now seemed committed to the leafy outlook of the North Shore rather than the Eastern Suburbs. This was perhaps the reason why William Henry's wife Mabel then purchased a large block of land at Britannia Avenue, Pennant Hills, which had a 132-feet frontage and a depth of 300 feet, for £118.[38]

Still a bachelor, by 1911 John Guy was a 'man about town' and generally the 'public face' of Ford Sherington. After two decades in Australia, Guy and his brother William were part of the employers' class who made up about five to six per cent of the adult male population in Sydney, as revealed in the 1911 Commonwealth census. And increasingly, they were seen as significant employers, with a growing workforce in their factory.

In mid-1911, Guy gave evidence to the New South Wales royal commission that had been set up to enquire into the alleged shortage of labour. This watershed enquiry had been set up in the context of the recent growth of factories in Sydney which were replacing the old craft establishments. Such change was associated with an apparent decline in boys undertaking apprenticeships while women began to prefer factory work to the tradi-

38 William George Sherington Memoirs.

tional areas of female employment such as domestic service. As such, the reports of the commission provide an understanding of the nature of manufacturing in Sydney which had expanded during the first decade of Federation with the benefit of tariff protection. Amongst the industries which the commission investigated was the leather trade. While Victoria was the major home of boots and shoes trade in Australia, other leather goods now had a foothold in New South Wales and the firm of the once Alfred Ford, now Ford Sherington, had become the dominant manufacturer.

The sole commissioner of this inquiry was A.B. Piddington, the most important judge in the industrial court. The extensive evidence Guy gave on 5 July 1911 revealed what the company had been producing since its move to Elizabeth Street and what comprised its labour force. It also indicated the nature of the manufacture of trunks as well as leather goods. While his brother William Henry had been the accountant of the firm, John Guy had actually worked on the factory floor and was more familiar with the changes in the manufacturing processes.[39] As Guy pointed out in his introductory remarks to the commission, the company made 'Leather bags, trunks, small leather goods'. Overall, the firm was involved in what was known in the trade as 'fancy leather goods'. Manufacture was divided into different departments. Sporting goods, such as footballs, were part of the business and a 'small ladies handbags' department had been opened recently. There were also fibre goods, and shipping trunks. Then there was the sheet metal section which comprised steel travelling trunks. Sheet metal work and tinsmithing was another department.[40]

39 Interview with William George Sherington.

40 *Interim Report of the Royal Commission of Inquiry into the Alleged Shortage of Labour in the State of New South Wales*, New South Wales Parliamentary Papers 1911–12, vol. II, 121.

In regard to the work force, the number of employees had grown fifty per cent in twelve months from about 109 in 1910 to 156 in 1911. Guy Sherington attributed this growth to the proximity of the factory to Central railway station which had just opened. This meant that 'the hands can leave their homes later; they can leave the station and be inside the factory, and working, within two minutes'. But the company had found it difficult to recruit skilled labour and were now seeking permits to bring in skilled men from Britain. It would seem that Alfred Ford and then Ford Sherington had become more reliant on female workers for leather work and male apprentices for tinsmithing. As Guy pointed out, when the company moved to Elizabeth Street in 1903, they had advertised for boys without success. 'So we conceived the idea of converting the very light side of our leather goods manufactures into a staff entirely staffed by girl labour'. Thus small leather goods were by 1911 made by 'girl labour'. But since it was apparently impossible to recruit adult journeymen in the buoyant labour market, the new company had also sought to employ boys as apprentices. And Guy Sherington emphasised that the company did train apprentices thoroughly and he wished to see them receive more formal education in Sydney Technical College (which was on the opposite side of Central station). The boys worked in the sheet metal-work department; although some of the smaller articles were made by machines, 'a very wide range' of human skills – which expensive machines had not yet been made to perform – were still in demand.[41]

Most of all, Guy Sherington's evidence emphasised the apparent shortage of skilled labour with the general expansion of industry in Sydney. Ford Sherington had at least eight or nine competitors making tin trunks. Unable to get skilled machinists for trunk making, the company had closed down certain departments and was even importing for sale such items as sporting goods. And as with William Pretty in Ipswich, Guy Sherington

41 Ibid., 121–22.

could claim that the company paid its workers well or at least the going rate (a claim generally supported in figures given to the commission) and that there were good working conditions – a special inspector had examined the area where women worked and there had been plenty of windows which let in light and overlooked the park opposite to Central railway. Equally he claimed an apprentice trained at Ford Sherington was well qualified and always in demand: he could leave the company and say: ' "I am a duly qualified apprentice of Ford Sherington's" and can sell his labour where he likes'.[42]

If this was the way of the future, there were those who believed that it undermined past practices that had been in colonial Sydney. The secretary of the Saddle and Harnessmakers and Leatherworkers' Union, himself a saddler – a trade requiring complex skills – told the commissioner that 'The general practice is to employ female and boy labour to do all the helping class of work. Ford and Sherington's are the greatest offenders in that direction'.[43] To such an old craftsman, modern methods of production were simply 'de-skilling' old trades such as his. But in many ways it was just what William Pretty had done in his factory at Ipswich where he had employed a female workforce and then broken down the production process so that it fitted methods of modern manufacturing.

As the new sole directors of Ford Sherington, John Guy and William Henry were obviously determined that the new enterprise would prosper. And the Prettys of Ipswich were there not only as providing models of production but financial support. Frank Pretty, who had just returned from Sydney, had helped to convince his father to continue the £800 guarantee even though William Pretty had been reluctant to do so, believing that he was growing too old for such commitments. However, William Pretty also warned William Sherington to be 'careful whose capital out-

42 Ibid., 122–25.
43 Ibid., 414.

side your own family you took in'.[44] He repeated the warning three months later when he suggested 'ordinary' shares remain in the hands of the family leaving 'preference' shares to outsiders:

> I would suggest that you do not let any outsiders have 'Ordinaries', or you may eventually lose control. Whether the outside public would take Prefs., even at 6% cumulative in such a small industrial, however good is questionable. If anything happened to yourself or brother who would be able to run the concern? No doubt when it has been established a few years longer they might, and no doubt you have someone coming into value. When folks invest in industrials there wants to be a stock exchange quotation in order they can realise.[45]

William Pretty had thereby outlined the dilemmas of many small manufacturing family firms in early-twentieth-century Australia. While the federal tariff helped sustain a market and protect sales, and pressure on government had led to the recruitment of skilled labour from Britain, there remained the question of capital for expansion. Industry depended significantly on the banking sector, much of which was British until the 1920s, while even Australian banks were dependent on British capital. Small businesses were restricted in access to bank finance, hence the importance of Frank Pretty's bank guarantee.[46] Small industrial firms were thus dependent on an embryonic almost informal capital market to raise funds for development and expansion. As William Pretty

---

44 Letter, William Pretty to 'dear Wm Sherrington', 21 February 1911 (Sherington Family Papers). Frank Pretty told William the new guarantee would also counter the influence of Ford who had mistakenly thought his father would not provide such a backing once Ford was out of the management.

45 Letter, William Pretty to 'dear Wm Sherington', 10 May 1911 (Sherington Family Papers).

46 Peter Cochrane, *Industrialisation and Dependence: Australia's Road to Economic Dependence* (St Lucia: University of Queensland Press, 1981), 59–61.

also recognised, it seemed best to keep control within the family even though this meant that management of the business also depended on stability within the family.

Some of these issues were portents for the future. For the present, there was prosperity in the years just before the First World War. In June 1911, William Henry reported to Frank Pretty that sales had grown fifty per cent in the seven months since the formation of Ford Sherington. As a result they had now ended the subtenancy arrangement and occupied the whole building they were leasing. But the landlord now wanted a fifty per cent increase for the renewal of the lease. Overall, their general location was very favourable as they found no trouble in attracting workers because of the short distance from Central railway station as well as from the tram terminus. As a result they decided to purchase a site nearby and build a new factory. What they wanted was a corner block preferably with a northerly aspect for good light, a size of approximately one hundred feet by one hundred feet. They also required an entrance that would give access from the street to the separate floors of the building, providing for economical working of stock. After three months of negotiations and by combining six blocks they had secured what they wanted – a factory site four minutes from where they were and eighty feet by 130 feet, giving 9000 square feet to each floor with a spare block adjoining thirty feet by eighty feet for yard for a total of £2445. Their bank had financed the purchase of the property on the assumption that the company had secured a cheap block of ground working out at fifteen pounds per foot. They had now nine months to arrange financing of the building which they were advised would cost £8000 to £9000 for five floors. This was double the space the company already had but they were considering renting two of the floors. Eventually an advance was secured by mortgage over land and buildings.

The new project thus created opportunities for finance from the Prettys and their investor friends. Reminding Frank of his previous reference to the 'safe investment of "Bricks and Mortar" ' William also wondered if he knew of anyone prepared to invest. They had decided to make this separate from the business, although the company would provide a sinking fund which could be done without straining the resources of the company, the projected interest on the mortgage being about £500 to £550 on the principal. The rents from the two floors to be leased would more than cover this interest, with each floor returning £400 to £500. After allowing for rates, taxes and insurance, the difference between such expenses and the sum to be paid as rent if they remained in present premises would be applied to a building sinking fund so after fifteen years they would have the prospects of providing for the original cost of land and buildings without 'trespassing too largely' on the company's profits or working capital. And if the building was financed by such a separate proposition they proposed to find a further sum for additions to plant by issuing preference shares for a limit of £2000. These one-pound shares were cumulative both as to capital and dividend carrying interest at six per cent with a bonus of one per cent after the ordinaries receives ten per cent and an additional one per cent if the ordinaries receive fifteen per cent, making a possible dividend of eight per cent. They thought this sufficiently 'liberal to induce investment' with 500 of these shares already taken up by a friend of the auditor. This investment along with William Pretty's continuing guarantee had allowed them to finance the large increase in sales. But William told Frank Pretty that they 'would issue these shares very cautiously and see that they are in the right proportion to the "Ordinaries" which are all held by the Sheringtons' in order that the management not be interfered with in any way by the votes of the "B" preference shares'. They would send William Pretty the current balance sheets and would follow his advice except that the company's shares were not to be listed 'on charge' – they could come back to that when the company was more established. But they would appreciate consideration of the proposal regarding the new site and perhaps Frank could refer this to any of his friends who were looking for a safe Australian investment. This would enable them to achieve their 'business ideal' of dealing with those who knew them personally while offering the English investor the 'certainty of careful and safe management' when those responsible for management held the ordinary shares for instance. Guy and William had both agreed to continue the 'active management' at the same remuneration of £250 per annum each and to look to dividends on the ordinaries to 'recoup and build up and increase the business'. They knew under what conditions the business had been and that 'safety combined with steady progress has been the policy adopted'.[47]

And so was born the factory site that would remain the home of Ford Sherington at Surry Hills for more than half a century. The move around the corner to build a new factory was part of a general change that was transforming the old suburb of Surry Hills into a place for modern factories alongside working class terraces and other housing for the poor. Previous forms of workshops were dying out and being replaced by factories and their machines. Light industry such as clothing and textiles, and leather and other manufacture such as that done by Ford Sherington, began to predominate. Amongst the so-called respectable classes there was a general view that the older inner-city working-class housing was inadequate, the entire city requiring remodelling to take into account new forms of transportation hailed by the opening of Central railway. The plague of 1902 in Sydney tended to reinforce these ideas. By 1905, Sydney Municipal Council had powers to resume and re-model for street widening, a process that probably affected Kippax Street. The new Lord Mayor Allen Taylor interpreted this to mean demolition of houses, and erection of factories and business premises. Giving evidence to the 1909 Royal Commission for the Improvement of the City of Sydney and its Suburbs, Taylor spoke of the need to improve traffic flow to Central, tramway access to the

47 Letter, 'Will' Sherington to Frank Pretty, 28 June 1911 (Sherington Family Papers).

Eastern Suburbs and of the 'enhancing effect' factories had on property rates.[48] Ford Sherington had chosen the right time to move.

Once again, the Prettys provided support from England. Annie Pretty, the wife of William and aunt of the three Sherington brothers in Australia, initially took up £1000 preference shares with William Pretty indicating he may put in a further £500 with the hope that they pay off one hundred or 200 per year, 'so as to get the concern entirely your own'.[49] With William Pretty now aged seventy-one, increasingly his son Frank had become spokesperson for his father in correspondence with his cousins. While Frank remained sceptical that any English investor would be interested in the building venture because it was such a long way off, especially considering that the same terms were offered on house mortgages in England, it was he who had persuaded his father to allow his mother, Annie, to take up 1000 'B' preference shares and, if necessary, a further 500 (subsequently taken up). He also finally persuaded his father, William, to continue his bank guarantee of £800 even though the older Pretty suggested that in view of his age they may need to make other arrangements in case he died. But Frank told William the Pretty family was unlikely to want back money from the 1500 preference shares unless the estate was wound up, when the capital may have to go into trust funds. Unlike his father, who wanted the Sherington brothers to reduce outside capital, Frank took the view 'I see that as the business grows you will want to introduce more Capital rather than pay off outside individuals'.[50] The Pretty family support for the Sherington venture in Australia was continuing into the next generation.

48 Christopher Keating, *Surry Hills: The City's Backyard* (Sydney: Hale and Iremonger, 1991), 69–74.
49 Letter, William Pretty to 'dear William', 9 October 1911 (Sherington Family Papers).
50 Letter, Frank Pretty to William Sherington, 25 January 1912 (Sherington Family Papers).

The purchase of the new building site had been completed by May 1911 through buying up cottages 125–27 Kippax Street and 9–15 Lacey Street, Surry Hills for £2445 of which the Bank of Australasia advanced £2300.[51] In April 1912, the company then purchased 84 Cooper Street for £2000, financed now by the issue of 'B' preference shares and a mortgage. By June, the tender for new building had been accepted. By December 1912 the building was complete, the overall project having cost £11,581 (only slightly in excess of the estimate of William Henry in his letter to Frank Pretty). The bank mortgage was £8400. The extra land purchased had provided an extra 12 000 square feet.[52] From April 1913, the registered office of Ford Sherington was Kippax and Lacey Streets, Surry Hills.

While still growing and prosperous in the years just prior to the First World War, Ford Sherington was not immune from the changing industrial climate. By the end of the first decade of Federation there were increasing moves towards industrial militancy in the general trade union movement. This was all part of conflict and tension between organised labour and organised capital, reflecting emerging class divisions in Australia. Indeed class conflict now emerged on the factory floor of Australian manufacturing than in the woolsheds as occurred in the shearers' strike in Queensland just after the Sheringtons arrived in Australia. The manufacturers and employers' associations, with which Ford Sherington was attached, were thus part of the new support for conservative politics and opposition to the Labor Party which was just coming to power in both the state and federal arena.[53] Almost defunct in the early 1890s, the New South Wales Chamber of Manufacturers was re-formed in 1895, and by

51 Ford Sherington Directors' Meeting Minutes, 15 May 1911.

52 Ford Sherington Directors' Meeting Minutes, 15 April 1912, 23 December 1912; Notes on History of Ford Sherington.

53 John Rickard, *Class and Politics: New South Wales, Victoria and the early Commonwealth* (Canberra: Australian National University Press, 1976), 167–203.

1899 had nearly 300 members. By 1901 there was concern over the new *Industrial Arbitration Act* and its possible effect on manufactures.[54] As a newly formed company Ford Sherington would soon play an important in this new politics of manufacturing and industrial relations.

As Guy Sherington had suggested to the 1911 enquiry, many of the workers in the company were females or young males. This may have had an effect on industrial relations in the company in that Ford Sherington was not involved in any major strikes or industrial disputes that marked many Sydney enterprises in 1913–14. But it was indirectly in conflict with industrial labour in its priority to import skilled male labour. Even before giving evidence to the 1911 royal commission, Guy Sherington, with other employers within the New South Wales Chamber of Manufacturers, had been pressing for more migrant labour to overcome labour shortages.[55] In August 1911 Ford Sherington had already received permission to import twelve trunk makers from Britain under a two-year employment contract and with wages higher than the award.[56] In the years leading up to the First World War, Guy Sherington became a leading figure in a state and national campaign to convince the federal Labor Government to allow the immigration of skilled workers while protecting Australian jobs through restricting imports via tariffs. In October 1912, Guy, now senior vice-president of the Chamber, along with other officials, highlighted a nation-wide Australian Manufacturers' Week through a tour of shop windows in the city where 'made in Australia' goods were on view.[57]

The overall prosperity of Ford Sherington now depended on a national market with the company having sales offices in many of the capital cities such as Brisbane. But sales fell in late 1911

---

54 Ibid., 167.
55 *Sydney Morning Herald*, 4 April 1911, 9.
56 *Sydney Morning Herald*, 5 August 1911, 5.
57 *Sydney Morning Herald*, 12 October 1912, 22.

as a result of a national shipping strike with no interstate shipments made in the last half of October.[58] Despite this setback, the directors of the company still had faith and hope in expansion, first in Sydney and then interstate. There still seemed to be plenty of profits, and now there was clear indication that a number of investors in Sydney were taking an interest in the company. In November 1912 Ford Sherington thus signed an agreement with 'Duncan Archibold McIntyre' (nominated as a 'gentleman') for 1500 'B' preference shares at a cost of 1500 pounds.[59] At the end of 1912 a dividend was declared at six per cent on 'B' preference shares and an interim dividend of twenty per cent on ordinary shares (mainly for Guy and William). There were also bonuses for employees and a sum set aside for a contingency fund.[60] In December 1913, it was also agreed to amend the agreement with Alfred Ford whereby he would continue to have £500 dividend per year for life on the 3000 'A' preference shares, provided Clara gave up, on the death of Alfred, the right to control raising of capital.[61] There was much buying of shares in the company during 1913–14 with participation not only from family members such as Arthur Sherington, but from those outside the family. This 'outside' investment was against the long offered advice of William Pretty but in the good times it seemed important to have more capital.

Not only did Ford Sherington have a new home, it was also developing new brand names, new outlets and even new production modes. Even before moving to the new factory site steps had been taken to register the 'Globe Brand' as part of the identification of leather goods which the firm manufactured.[62] It is not entirely clear why this brand name had been chosen except for the obvious association with the idea of global travel. And so it

58 Ford Sherington Directors' Meeting Minutes, 20 November 1911.
59 Ford Sherington Directors' Meeting Minutes, 8 November 1912.
60 Ford Sherington Directors' Meeting Minutes, 23 December 1912.
61 Notes on History of Ford Sherington.
62 Ford Sherington Directors' Meeting Minutes, 19 June 1911.

would seem the famous Globite suitcase was born, soon to be made not out of leather but of reinforced fibre. By July 1914, the company had thus resolved to register 'Globite' and 'Beatzall' in the fibre suitcase section and 'Fordite' in the leather section.[63] The catalogues of the company's products which were produced over the next decade, however, placed an emphasis on the general 'Globe Brand' of high-grade leatherware, fibre cases and trunks, sports goods and belts as well as steel trunks and metalware. Essentially, Ford Sherington had incorporated the old metal trunk business of Alfred Ford into the making of products such as travel goods and sporting equipment, which involved the use of leather and fibre.[64]

In order to sell these products the company began to open new salesrooms, the first being Leith House at 127 York Street in Sydney from May 1913. Then in July 1913 a salesroom was opened in the Australian Building on the corner of Flinders Lane and Elizabeth Street, Melbourne. In January 1914 an agent was appointed in Perth. The company then went into production in Brisbane from May 1914 and in Adelaide from July 1914.[65]

The company was still small enough to reach out to staff. During the early 1900s, the company had held a number of staff picnics. In December 1913, the staff at Ford Sherington felt confident to hold its first annual dinner and smoking concert. The chairman of proceedings was Arthur Platt who would become a long standing employee of the company as the general manager of production. The importance of Arthur Platt to the new company was seen in the decision in 1911, just after the formation of Ford Sherington, to allot to him 100 'B' preference shares on the basis of ten shares for every year of service and that a bonus of one pound per £1000 sales in the leather department be paid to him when he was foreman of that department. The dividend and

63 Notes on History of Ford Sherington.
64 Ford Sherington Manufacturers Australia, Catalogue, c.1918.
65 Ford Sherington Directors' Meeting Minutes, 1913–14.

bonus was to be paid each half year.[66] By May 1914, Arthur Platt had been appointed factory superintendent, and he held this position throughout the difficult years ahead.

The First World War and its Aftermath

The war fractured families in so many ways. In Suffolk, following the example of his father, Frank Pretty had been active in the army reserve being commissioned from 1900 as a lieutenant, rising to captain in 1903 and to major in 1912. On the outbreak of war, then aged thirty-six, Frank joined the fourth battalion of the Suffolk regiment which had absorbed the earlier voluntary territorials. In accordance with the custom of the Suffolk Territorials, and the traditions of fox hunting, Frank took his horse to war, bringing to mind the film *War Horse* (2011) produced almost a century later. His younger brother, Donald, aged only twenty-one, also enlisted as an officer in the Suffolk regiment which was soon involved in the early battles of the war. After a brief period of leave in London, in March 1915 Donald was hospitalised with jaundice. On 26 April 1915 (the day after the Anzacs landed at Gallipoli) Frank was wounded in the Battle of St Julien. Then in May 1915 Donald was seriously wounded by shell fire while in the trenches at Neuve Chapelle. He died without regaining consciousness and was buried in France in accordance with military custom.[67]

Within a year, William Pretty had died at Ipswich – on 12 February 1916 – attracting a large funeral procession and many tributes. His wife Annie lived into the 1920s. Frank continued to serve throughout the war as a Major, becoming second in command of his battalion. He was wounded in the elbow at Ypres in 1916 and was later mentioned in dispatches. After the war, he

66 Ford Sherington Directors' Meeting Minutes, 1911.
67 Pretty Family Papers (courtesy of Mark Shephard).

continued to maintain an interest in the wellbeing of the men in his battalion, being described as 'a steady, kind, reliable man, very much liked in East Suffolk where he did much welfare work for the 4th battalion of the Suffolk regiment'.[68]

Following the death of William Pretty the corset business of William Pretty and Sons went into decline, unable to survive in the changing market of women's underwear with corsets becoming less fashionable in the world of the flapper in the 1920s. The 'outworker' factories began to close. In 1927 the Footman Pretty store in Ipswich was taken over by Debenham & Peabody. In 1930 William Pretty and Sons went into liquidation. R. & W.H. Symington's of Market Harborough acquired the business and renamed it William Pretty & Sons Ltd but with no involvement by the Pretty family. Courtauld's acquired the business in 1968 but closed the factory in Ipswich in 1982. A new outlet under the name of Rowley continued to manufacture maternity wear and children's clothes.[69]

The First World War thus helped to end the close association the Sheringtons had with the Prettys in Suffolk. Increasingly, it was also local circumstances that now influenced the development of Ford Sherington. In Australia, at the beginning of the First World War, Guy Sherington was caught up in a national industrial dispute. Now a vice-president of the New South Wales Chamber of Manufactures, he acted as an arbitrator with other Australian chambers of manufacturing which had been angered by the decision of the Commonwealth Department of Defence to allow trade union officials access to industrial sites which were fulfilling defence contracts. Guy and William Vicars, the president of the New South Wales Chamber sympathised with their fellow manufacturers but believed that 'this was not the time, when

68 Pretty Correspondence (courtesy of Mark Shephard); Skelcher and Durrant, *Edith Pretty*, 28–31.
69 Clark and Munting, *Suffolk Enterprises*, 98; research of Roger Kennell.

the Empire was at war, to fight the Defence Department'. After George Pearce, the Minister for Defence, had agreed to modify the arrangements restricting union access to site, in February 1915 Guy Sherington chaired a meeting of members in New South Wales explaining that while the executive of the New South Wales Chamber still found the arrangements objectionable, the 'truest patriotism' was to help the department equip the troops and tender for supplies as usual. That view seemed to prevail throughout Australia despite the continuing strong objections of the South Australian Chamber of Manufactures.[70]

In September 1915, both Guy and Arthur enlisted in the Australian Imperial Force (AIF). In the wake of the Gallipoli campaign, there was a general surge in numbers of Australian men joining the army; in New South Wales there were often recruiting marches from the country to the city. While the recruiting surge died off in 1916 – leading to the conscription referenda campaigns – the enlistment patterns of 1914–15 laid the basis whereby forty per cent of the male population aged eighteen to forty-five would enlist in what was, along with that of New Zealand, one of only two voluntary armies to fight on the Western Front. Aged respectively thirty-nine and thirty-seven on enlistment, both Arthur and Guy were amongst the small proportion of over thirty-five year olds who enlisted. But their army careers would be very different.

Before enlisting Arthur had spent a period of four months in the Waverley Rifle Club (he was then living at 'Stoneleigh' on York Road, Waverley). His initial training as a gunner was in the Royal National Park south of Sydney. Soon promoted to corporal, by early 1916 he was in France on his way to becoming a second lieutenant, then lieutenant, and later joining the Australian Fourth Field Artillery Brigade in August. On 25 August 1916 he suffered multiple shell wounds which eventually led to

70 C.R. Hall, *The Manufacturers: Australian Manufacturing Achievements to 1960* (Sydney: Angus & Robertson, 1971), 296–98.

the amputation of his left index finger. He also suffered other minor wounds to his upper left arm, back, left thigh and head. After being in hospital for a number of weeks he did return to his unit for a while but for most of the rest of the war he was generally involved in matters of army administration, while formally attached to the Second Divisional Ammunition Column. In November 1917, he was transferred to AIF headquarters in London, returning on occasions to France but spending much of his time in England. At the end of the war, he was granted leave with pay and allowances in February 1919 to investigate the condition of leather and sheet metal goods under an arrangement with Messrs McEwen and Co. of Cannon Street London. In March 1919, he was granted leave of absence without pay or allowance returning to Australia via America on the *Baltic* (and arriving in Sydney without apparently informing his family in advance). By this time he had already formed a romantic attachment to Olive Marie Hingley, of London. In 1920 Arthur returned to marry Olive at the fashionable church of St Martin's in the Fields Trafalgar Square with Frank Pretty as groomsman.[71]

Guy Sherington had a more spectacular career in the war. He had enlisted with Arthur and also spent his initial training as a gunner at the Royal National Park camp. By March 1916, he was second lieutenant and then lieutenant. By then he was already being given special attention and coming under notice of those attached to AIF headquarters in London for his well-developed managerial skills. By September 1916 he was promoted to staff captain. He was absent on special duties in France for a few weeks in February and March 1917. By September 1917 he had been promoted to major, perhaps because of coming to the attention of military authorities. Recognition of his administrative skills was seen in his being involved in administering the 1916 con-

71 Attestation Enlistment File of Arthur Sherington, National Archives of Australia; Letter, Olive Sherington to Richard Sherington, 1970.

scription referenda amongst the troops as well as the 1917 federal election.

His proposals for the demobilisation and repatriation of the troops then brought Guy prominence and national attention. First, he argued for a small staff to think out the stages of repatriation. Then in February 1918, he was appointed to organise a Demobilisation and Repatriation Section for this purpose. Keeping in touch with the British War Office he then presented a report on the problem and in subsequent papers he developed proposals which would form the basis for the Australian repatriation scheme. From August 1918 he became Staff Officer for Repatriation and Demobilisation.[72]

While in England Guy had met Beatrice Maud Antell, aged twenty-nine, who was the daughter of a mechanical engineer. They were wed in the Hendon Wesleyan church in London on 27 February 1919. And as if to impose the known present upon the imagined past Guy listed the occupation of his now long deceased father William Charles on the marriage certificate as 'Fancy Goods Buyer'. Five days later the newlyweds sailed for Australia on the *Euripides*.[73] A month later on his return to Australia, Guy was awarded the newly established Order of the British Empire for his services in the war.

The Chamber of Manufactures in New South Wales gave 'Major Guy Sherington' an honorary lunch in May 1919. Guy's views mirrored what historians have described as those of 'Empire loyalists'. Born in England, he was committed to the British Empire. With his close affiliations with employers' associations, and having experienced prewar industrial unrest, he may also have been close in views to those who saw communism as a po-

---

72 Attestation Enlistment File of Guy Sherington, National Archives of Australia; C.E.W. Bean, *Official History of Australia in the War of 1914–1918*, vol. VI (Sydney: Angus & Robertson, 1954), 1054; Hall, *The Manufacturers*, 297.

73 Attestation Enlistment File of Guy Sherington, National Archives of Australia.

tential threat in the wake of the 1917 Russian Revolution. Such views were often shared by the officer class who had served in the war. [74] Guy chose the occasion of his honorary lunch to talk about matters of Empire and the lessons of war. He praised the British prime minister Lloyd George as 'a brilliant statesman', but indicated that he 'could not believe for a moment that the League of Nations could guarantee future peace' and so each nation should 'be prepared'. Moreover, 'He thought that the business-men of Australia should be formed into a corps, so that if trouble occurred they would be able to undertake administrative work'.[75] Undoubtedly some at the lunch might have seen this as a call to arms with more relevance to domestic Australian politics and industrial relations than to international events. Indeed it was the sort of language that D.H. Lawrence probably encountered from ex-army officers in 1921, leading him to write the novel *Kangaroo* with its overtones of right-wing secret armies working to bring down the communist trade union leaders.[76]

At home the war had a major impact on the Australian economy. Inflation rose to ten per cent a year from 1912–13 to 1919–20. At the same time, in common with most other European economies, real gross domestic product fell.[77] The pre-war years of sustained economic growth in manufacturing seemed to be over. Whilst his two brothers were at the war, William Henry Sherington had continued to manage the affairs of Ford Sherington with some assistance from Alfred Ford. From as early as 1916 it was decided to subsidise the wages of employees who had enlisted by making up the difference between factory and military pay.[78] The large number of female employees

74 Andrew Moore, *The Right Road: A History of Right-Wing Politics in Australia* (Melbourne: Oxford University Press, 1995), 23–35.
75 *Sydney Morning Herald*, 23 May 1919, 8.
76 Robert Darroch, *D.H. Lawrence in Australia* (Sydney: Macmillan, 1921).
77 Butlin, Barnard and Pincus, *Government and Capitalism*, 74–75.
78 Ford Sherington Directors' Meeting Minutes, 28 January 1916.

Ford Sherington Balance Sheet 1916

Liabilities		Assets	
Nominal capital 50 000 shares less unissued 25 750	£24 250	Cash, book debts, bonds, investments	£11 423
Creditors	£10 670	Stock, plant machinery	£25 513
Mortgagees	£15 550	Land and buildings	£19 920
Outstanding liabilities	£789	Goodwill and patents	£2005
Provision for contingencies	£6959	Profit/loss acc	£951

probably meant that the company still retained much of its workforce. But despite the wartime demand for leather products such as boots for the Indian Army, there was continuing general industrial unrest culminating in the General Strike of unionists in 1917. The company itself was caught up in a federal award case brought on by the Leather Workers' Employees Union leading to legal expenses associated with the case arising from the legal expenses of the Leathergoods' Employers Association.[79]

Despite these difficulties, the balance sheet at the end of 1916 suggests that William Henry was managing the company competently without engaging in any new expansion.

On these figures, the company was still able to pay a dividend of six per cent on 'B' preference shares with a bonus of two per cent and a dividend of ten per cent on ordinary shares. By the end of 1917 the profit had declined to £551 but there were now further provision for contingencies, suggesting the hand of fin-

79 Ford Sherington Directors' Meeting Minutes, 19 April 1918.

ancial caution. Towards the end of the war, the company began planning for the possible return of normal economic conditions with the coming of peace. By the end of 1918, the company was in formal contact with Guy Sherington in Britain, having sent him £4000 for the purchase of fibre and other large purchases for 1918–19.[80]

The worry of virtually running the business by himself, albeit with some help from Alfred Ford, seems to have a marked effect on the health of William Henry. On doctor's advice, and following the return of Guy from the war, he decided to take an extended holiday in late 1919 and relocated his now large family to Bowral in the Southern Highlands. Originally intended as a break for six months, the stay became four and a half years. Already marked by strong class distinction, Bowral was then a town where many prominent Sydney businessmen had holiday houses and their own local Royal Bowral Golf Club, which excluded the local tradesmen who had to found their own golf club for the 'townies'. After his six months extended holiday from late 1919 to early 1920 William Henry developed a pattern of getting to work. He travelled to Sydney on a Monday, stayed overnight at the Sydney Hotel, returned to Bowral on the Tuesday night, spent Wednesday in Bowral, and then repeated the process, having Thursday and Friday once again at the office in Kippax Street.[81]

Living in a small Bowral cottage, 'Wyloe', which the family had purchased, the Sherington children now grew up with new chums such as Rex Boardman, and Don Bradman and his future wife Jessie Menzies both of whom would become friends of the Sherington family for many years, and particular lifelong correspondents for William George and Dorothy. (The young William George even played cricket with Don in the Bradman family's backyard against the now famous 'tank stand' where he practised

80 Ford Sherington Directors' Meeting Minutes, Balance Sheet, December 1917; 17 October 1918.
81 William George Sherington Memoirs.

all his skills – 'you couldn't bowl out "Braddie" only catch him'). A new family car – an Overland Tourer – added to the delights of country living. The elder children Ada, William and Dorothy were sent off in 1920 to boarding schools in Sydney and the Blue Mountains. There was also the tragic early death in 1922 of Marjorie, the youngest of the three Sherington daughters.[82]

The return of Guy Sherington raised questions about the future directions of the company and the roles that each of the brothers would now play as well as other staff. The end of war had brought some prospects of prosperity despite the difficult conditions during the war. There was the good prospect of British investment as Britain turned more to its Empire for trade and a possible source of profits. While much attention focused on rural development and creation of agricultural exports, from 1921 the Australian government also sought to encourage Australian manufacturing through tariffs, which were built on the pre-1914 system of protection but with associated preferential tariff arrangements for goods from Britain. Increasingly, the system became complicated by the patterns of inflation in Britain and elsewhere helping to give some imports an advantage over Australian manufacturing despite the formal tariff. A Commonwealth Tariff Board was created to regulate the system and hear disputes. By the end of the 1920s reviews and more legislation led to Australia having one of the highest tariff rates and most complicated systems for imported goods in the world.[83] At the same time industrial relations and the labour market in the 1920s had become increasingly regulated through the arbitration system and wage decisions.[84]

The immediate postwar strategy of Ford Sherington in the years 1919–22 was twofold. First, the company continued the prewar expansion into new sites of production and new markets,

82 William George Sherington Memoirs.
83 Butlin et al., *Government and Capitalism*, 88–90.
84 Ibid., 98–103.

building up manufacturing in Melbourne and Brisbane and appointing sales agents in China and New Zealand and even exporting to Java. Second, the company vigorously sought to protect the 'Globe' leather case and the new 'Globite' fibre suitcase brand, ensuring the supply of soft fibre for production and taking steps to register the name overseas in Britain and America and prosecuting those locally who sought to use the name illegally. The value of products sold doubled from 1918 to 1921.[85] On this basis, it was decided to increase the formal capital from 50 000 to 100 000 shares. In June 1923, a further issue of 5000 shares was initiated.[86]

Driving many of these initiatives were the views of Guy. In 1921 he went once again to Britain for an extended period. On return to Australia, he recommended that the company make arrangements with a Swedish mill to supply soft fibre on the same basis that had been arranged with the company Spaulding in the US on a trip he had apparently made in 1914. He also made suggestions to maintain supplies from Germany and to give special attention to such matters as handbag and other frames and fittings. He also saw an opportunity to buy a leather-measuring machine, lock dies and draw on army-surplus sales. His report covered such matters as patents, advertising, exhibitions of products, and fashions in belts and handbag styles.[87]

During the war Guy was a gifted administrator and very adept at seeing and seizing opportunities. His status and stature in the Sydney community was built on his prewar contacts in such organisations as the New South Wales Chamber of Commerce. Now there was the national recognition he had achieved through the award of the OBE. Guy was an entrepreneur, very experienced in the industrial production and marketing of Ford Sherington goods. He was in this way much like his uncle William Pretty.

---

85 Ford Sherington Accounts.
86 Ford Sherington Directors' Meeting Minutes, June 1923.
87 Ford Sherington Directors' Meeting Minutes, 6 December 1921.

But unlike William Pretty he seems to have been a potential risk taker. In contrast, his elder brother William Henry was a cautious man, an accountant who was now not inclined to take risk possibly because of his extensive family and the financial commitments this brought. William Henry was also very aware of the company's commitments to the 'outside shareholders', which complicated matters further, particularly in view of the prewar warning from William Pretty that the family should always retain control (even though the family itself was now dividing). But the balance between ordinary and preference shareholders was now changing. Over the 1920s, the number of ordinary shares on issue remained at 24 600 but the number of preference shares grew to 45 550.[88]

In these contexts there were also personal difficulties emerging within the Sherington family. William Henry's wife Mabel Helen did not like the attitudes of the new English wives of Arthur and Guy. She had never interfered in the running of the company and now she saw English wives with English ways doing so. And then there was even the suggestion from the new wives that in England owner managers only came in when it suited them, otherwise leaving the running of the company to employed staff.[89]

It was coming down to who would run the company and which strategy would direct its future. The dual directorship of William Henry and Guy initiated at the founding of the company was modified somewhat in the postwar years. In June 1921, it had been decided to allocate specific roles of management. William Henry would be in charge of finance and delivery supervision. Guy would assume the oversight of sales, sales agencies and advertising. As a new working director, Arthur Platt would be in charge of factories and sub-factories. Arthur Sherington was also periodically on the board of directors even though he remained

88 Ford Sherington Accounts and Records.
89 Interview with William George Sherington.

as William Pretty and Sons' representative in Australia.[90] The roles of each director became significant as economic conditions became more difficult with increasing competition, despite growing sales. Efforts to maintain the high price of the Globite in the face of competition were also coming under pressure.

Amidst all these concerns, there was a significant change in the living arrangements for William Henry and Mabel Sherington. In 1924 William Henry, Mabel Helen and their family moved into their new house 'Bramhall' in Britannia Street, Pennant Hills. The move to Pennant Hills had taken a decade. In 1909 Mabel had purchased three quarters of an acre on the Blackacre Estate in Britannia Street, Pennant Hills. In 1916 she purchased an adjoining lot and in 1917 William Henry bought a further adjoining lot. In 1920, the land was still planted with fruit trees. They now built a large brick house of ten rooms with a dominating gable roof of small terracotta tiles. The style of the house as well as the name seemed to have strong English or even East Anglian associations, given William Henry's Suffolk ancestry and Mabel's long family lineage with Essex. Set on two acres and costing £4000 to build, it was expensive but large enough for a family of eight and a live-in servant.[91] After more than two decades of marriage, Mabel had a home where her family would live for the next three decades. For future generations of Sheringtons, it would become known simply as 'Grandma's'.

The year 1924 was also a watershed in another way. Just as the immediate postwar boom was coming to an end a crisis was emerging in Ford Sherington. Matters of dispute came to head when Alfred Ford, who still chaired the directors' meetings and still called himself 'managing director', decided to step down. He nominated as his successor William Henry – being the brother who had been longest in the business. Guy objected strongly.

---

90 Ford Sherington Directors' Meeting Minutes, 23 June 1921.
91 Helen Barker, *Houses of Hornsby Shire,* vol. II (Sydney: Hornsby Shire Historical Society, 1998), 82–84.

The matter went to the 1924 annual meeting of the company where it was proposed that William Henry be general manager for twelve months, leading to objections on legal grounds but hopes that there could be agreement between the two brothers. An adjourned annual general meeting and then a special extraordinary meeting moved to appoint a fifth director who could mediate differences. Guy nominated Sir Robert Cairns Anderson, a prominent former New South Wales government bureaucrat and now Sydney businessman, while William Henry put forward the company solicitor A.J. McLachlan who was eventually elected chair after Cairns Anderson withdrew. For a period Alexander McLachlan chaired the board of directors but by April 1925 Arthur Sherington had taken over as chair with McLachlan also resigning as a director.[92]

These matters obviously shocked the Sydney business community – a successful firm now riven by disputes between the two brothers who had worked so hard for more than three decades to make it a success. It also affected the Sherington family with Ada Caroline feeling that she could do little even though each of her sons constantly sought her advice and perhaps support for their differing positions. Having helped to establish the business she did not want to see this conflict as a legacy for the family.[93]

For the next three years, from 1925 to the end of 1927, there was an uneasy 'peace' between William Henry and Guy as economic conditions became more difficult. With increasing competition in the market, constant attention was paid to overheads and costs, even though the sales projections for 1925 was over £150 000. At the end of 1926, it was finally decided to offer the position of general manager to Guy. Still entrepreneurial in outlook, he was now considering a new venture in the context of the 1920s housing expansion in the suburbs of Australian cities. In

92 Ford Sherington Directors' Meeting Minutes, October 1924 to April 1925, passim.
93 Interview with William George Sherington.

1927, he had brought out from England six electric stoves with the idea of such manufacture by Ford Sherington at a time when only gas stoves were in use in Australia.[94]

These events were soon interrupted by a series of personal crises within the family. On 9 June 1927, nurse Alice Banfield, aged sixty-one, died in a private hospital in Manly. Her death seemed a portent for change, coming almost four decades after she had arrived as the 'pioneer' for the Banfield–Sherington party of immigrants. Six months later, on 30 December 1927, William Henry Sherington, aged fifty-three, died suddenly at home in Pennant Hills. His eldest son, William George Sherington, now joined the company, having already left school early to train as an accountant at the firm Smith Johnson with general aim of helping manage the family finances. And just six months later, Guy Sherington, aged forty-nine, died just after being ordered to take a rest because of his heart condition.

The death of her youngest sister and then of two of her three sons in the space of twelve months must have been devastating for Ada Caroline. For Ford Sherington the loss of the two directors who had guided the company since its formation was a major blow. There were also complications with their affairs because of the close financial relationship that had existed between the two brothers and the company since its foundation, often involving individual loans to Ford Sherington. Overall, much of the brothers' capital was tied up in the business. In August 1928 Arthur Sherington came on to the board as general manager but was obviously not prepared to assume the mantle of his brothers at his age in life. Within six months he had resigned as general manager and left the board in August 1929, almost on the eve of the 1930s Depression, after which 'he terminated all interests and connections with the Company'.[95]

94 Ibid.
95 William George Sherington Memoirs.

The next decade marked the passing of most of those who had arrived from England or had laid the foundations of Ford Sherington. In February 1931, Alfred Ford fell ill with prostate cancer. After nursing him for almost a fortnight his wife Clara Jane caught pneumonia and died of heart failure in the Manly private hospital aged seventy-four on 13 February 1931, just eleven days before the death of her husband. On 11 April 1936, Ada Caroline Sherington, aged eighty-four, died at Manly. Her second-born son, Arthur Charles Sherington, died at Collaroy in September 1938 after a long illness. All the three Sherington brothers were now dead after a half century in Australia, though they left behind a legacy of enterprise which would extend for another forty years.

It was the three Sherington brothers' wives who would survive throughout the 1930s Depression and into the prosperity of the post-1945 period. Two were widows with children. New Zealand-born Mabel Helen had to care for a young family without the certainty of a regular income, with so much of the family capital tied up with Ford Sherington. (And for his own, unknown, reasons, her husband had provided that she would only remain a beneficiary in his will provided she did not marry again.) Parts of the Pennant Hills property were sold in 1929 and 1933, reducing the land to only an acre. Mabel remained there with her eldest daughter Ada; they later moved to Epping in 1953. It was not quite the original 'Grandma's place' but 'Grandma' continued to preside over family gatherings in ways that some found cruel and manipulative but perhaps understandable in view of what she had to endure with the early death of William Henry. She died in 1968, two years after the death of her daughter Ada.

Guy's English-born wife Beatrice had two young sons, Peter and Ian, aged under ten when their father died. She now struggled to bring them up. She began to drink heavily and when she did not pay her accounts, suppliers forwarded them to Ford Sherington. Soon an alcoholic she had to seek the help of family including English-born Olive, wife of Arthur Sherington, who had no children although did have some commitments to her own family in Britain. Olive took over the care of young Peter and Ian while Beatrice spent some time in hospital.[96] Beatrice died in a private hospital in 1952.

From the mid-1930s Olive was an active if not merry widow. Having continued her friendship with Edith Pretty, she returned to England on a number of occasions and, as noted at the beginning of this book, was present at the Sutton Hoo dig in 1939. She had always been an active woman. During the Second World War, she drove the last ambulance out of the south of France to escape to Britain. She had then received the Britain Order of Merit award. At the end of the war she had returned to Australia, feted as a war heroine, with a swag of medals and unit colours to show the Sherington family. In 1947 Olive was on the same ship taking the postwar Wallaby team to Britain, securing the signatures of team members for her young great nephew. She never remarried but finally retired to Canberra to live on investments and avoid federal death duties. She was a fount of knowledge on the history of the family, some of which now seems inaccurate and even misleading, but she also defended the Sherington family into which she had married.[97]

An Australian Family Company

The family firm had been handed on not so much as a treasure but as a legacy which could become a burden. Family finances were closely linked to family fortunes which could not be realised. It may not have been their choice, but the Sheringtons born in Australia were now tied into a venture of their fathers and

---

96 Ibid.

97 Diaries of O.M. Sherington, British Women's Mechanical Corps Australian War Memorial 749/93/1; Certificate and Cuttings of Mrs Olive Marie Sherington, Australian War Memorial PR 83/207.

grandmother. The unexpected transfer between the English-born and the Australian-born came on the eve of the 1930s Depression with the spectre of mass unemployment and little economic growth for a decade. A company which had once been seen as guaranteeing profits could not even pay a dividend during the early 1930s.

The immediate tasks were to secure both family and company. This was particularly crucial for the family William Henry Sherington had left behind. Still only a young man himself aged in his early twenties, William George Sherington sought the help of Ray Moore, a senior partner of Smith Johnson, where they had gotten to know one another. He persuaded Moore to join Ford Sherington from April 1928, but the initial task was to reorganise family finances. The income of the family had depended on William Henry's fees as a director, then £1500, as well as dividends on 10 500 ordinary shares and 2101 preference shares then paying two per cent and six per cent respectively but soon to be suspended because of the Depression. Overall, William Henry's annual income had been £ 2250 pounds. The prospects were now much reduced. The Ford Sherington board of directors gave his wife Mabel Helen Sherington half the director's fees for one year as an act of grace, but then the financial future was uncertain. William George was at least employed in the company with a good salary. His sister Ada went into nursing, training first at Royal Prince Alfred and then the Children's Hospital at Camperdown, where she remained until 1935. His other sister Dorothy took up typing and office work. But the three younger sons were still in school with the youngest, Donald, holding a scholarship at Fort Street Boys' High School. There were savings at home with the live-in domestic help let go and controls on family expenses. The family sold the 1918 Overland car as well as three blocks of land at Oyster Bay on the Georges River. Twenty acres of land held at Bowral were sold back to the original owner, Ted Boardman. Of most significance was the decision to refinance the mortgage on the Britannia Street home which still stood at £2250 to the Bank of Australasia which now sought repayment. With the help of Ray Moore, arrangements were made for the Australian Mutual Provident (AMP) society to take over the mortgage with quarterly payments.[98]

It was a similar form of cooperation that marked the new management at Ford Sherington. By April 1930, William was managing director on the board of the company. The close relationship between 'Bill' Sherington and Ray Moore, later to be board chairman, would become a feature of the operation of the company for the next four decades. In contrast to the conflict between Guy and William Henry there was now careful management of company affairs in a difficult economic climate. There was none of the entrepreneurial flair of Guy but rather the caution of those trained in accounting procedures, with a clear and growing understanding of the travel goods market. There was also the chairman Maxwell Allen who had knowledge of accounts, while the long-time staff member Arthur Platt maintained a clear direction on the factory floor. By the mid-1930s, the fortunes of the company had recovered to the degree that regular dividends could be reinstituted.

From the mid-1930s, personal life could now take precedence over company affairs. The Australian-born children of William Henry and Helen began to find their own life partners. In June 1934, Bill Sherington married Marjorie Frances Johnson of Camden. They came to live at Roseville, soon building their own house in Park Avenue costing £1650 including land and financed through a £250 deposit and two loans over ten and fifteen years. This was not a reminder of Suffolk or even London housing but rather inter-war Australian red brick – albeit with some art deco features such as the window frames:

> We had a solid brick cavity wall [and a] tile roof with stone foundations incorporating an under house garage, front ver-

98 William George Sherington Memoirs.

> andah, three bedrooms, two side verandahs, lounge room, dining room, kitchen bath & shower with toilet, outside laundry with toilet. Later we enclosed the western verandah – the eastern verandah was built enclosed.[99]

Living at Roseville from 1935, Bill and Marjorie had four children: David (born in1935), Bruce (born in 1937), Elizabeth (born in 1939) and Geoffrey (born in 1945). Through her mother's side of the family, Marjorie was descended from the retailer immigrant Joseph Thompson who had arrived in Australia in 1834 with twelve children who helped him to establish a commercial business, parts of which would later become entwined with the David Jones retail empire. Marjorie Johnson's grandfather John Thompson was, in 1907, the senior director of David Jones. Like his own grandfather and father, he was a stalwart of the Congregational Church in Sydney. His house in Victoria Street, Ashfield still stands. [100]

Dorothy Sherington, the second-born daughter of William Henry and Mabel Helen, married Alan Chambers, nephew of the Anglican Bishop Chambers, founder of Trinity Grammar School, Alan later became company secretary of Concrete Industries but died of cancer in his early fifties. Dorothy and Alan had three children Helen (born in 1937), Malcolm (born in 1941) and Barbara (born in 1943), all of whom graduated from university with initial degrees respectively in the professions of medicine, engineering and physiotherapy – the first family group of university graduates in this second Australian-born generation.

The younger Sherington males also married during the late 1930s and 1940s. Charles Sherington married Nea Pearce in Sydney. He then moved south to become managing director of a branch of Ford Sherington in Melbourne. Having settled in Mel-

---

99 William George Sherington Memoirs.

100 Chris Patten, 'Northridge Victoria Street', *Ashfield History*, no. 14; Journal of the Ashfield and District Historical Society, April 2003, 113–24.

bourne, Charles and Nea had three children Richard (born in 1940) Annette (born in 1942) and Grant (born in 1945).

Charles's twin brother Frank enlisted in the Sixth Division AIF in 1940 along with his second cousin Peter Sherington, the son of Guy. They served in the Middle East and New Guinea. Frank returned from the war to marry Phyllis Duesbury. They had two postwar babies – Helen (born in 1946) and Kay (born in 1950).

The youngest of the children of William Henry and Mabel Helen, Donald, had remained in school to complete his studies at Fort Street High School before undertaking accountancy exams. In 1942, he became part of the Australian Military Forces sent to New Guinea. Of all the Sherington males, his wartime experience had a major psychological impact and he found it difficult to adjust to the early years of peace. As with other Australian soldiers, it was probably post-traumatic stress disorder as we now describe the effect of the emotional and psychological scars of war. After the war, he agreed to go to South Africa to begin a branch of the company in Port Elizabeth (an idea which the factory manager Arthur Platt had first proposed in the 1930s). In South Africa he married Edith Bolton who was of English parentage. She later became part of the famous 'black sash' movement of mainly women of English heritage who demonstrated against the apartheid regime. Don and Edith had two children Donald, who was born in 1946, and Evelyn, who was born in 1951 and killed in a car accident in 1968.

Throughout the war, Bill Sherington remained as managing director in Sydney, although he was also involved for a period in the war as a captain in signals communication in Western Australia from May 1942. The end of the Second World War brought the prospect of new opportunities for Ford Sherington. The branch factory at Brisbane had been formed after the war, under Bill Mitchell who would soon come to Sydney. There were also outlets at Adelaide and Perth. This was the extension of Ford

Sherington which would soon be complemented by the move to South Africa.

The expansion of factory outlets and the prospects of increased production allowed for the postwar restructure of Ford Sherington. William Henry and Guy had created a limited liability company in which control resided in the family. Since their death family members had become increasingly involved. But the company also had commitments to the extensive number of preference shareholders. By becoming a public company listed on the stock exchange this would allow more flexibility including the prospects of capital raising or even family members eventually realising capital gains from all the years of family involvement.

In December Ford Sherington Holdings was formed under the *Companies Act 1874* (NSW). There was a subscribed capital of 400 000 issued ordinary shares at 5/- (principally in the hands of the Sherington family) and 45 500 shares issued to holders of preference shares of Ford Sherington Limited. The company was also selling 133,328 ordinary shares so as to achieve a wider distribution of capital and so that the company could become a public company for the purposes of the *Income Tax Assessment Act 1936* (Cwlth) and to enable it to qualify to list on the stock exchange. The public was informed that 'The management of the Company is still in the hands of the original founders – the Sherington family'.[101]

The new shares were soon eagerly sought but rarely gained in this new successful public company. By the end of the 1950s there were 'complaints' in the 'financial press' that a 'death adder had taken up residence in the company till'. The company continued to pay an 'unrelenting' ten per cent dividend but there had been no share capital issues and no prospects of those occurring. There was also no adjustment on the exchange rate between Australia and South Africa where the factory in South Africa was probably

101 Memorandum to clients relating to the sale of shares in Ford Sherington Holdings Limited, Ford Sherington Documents.

providing £10 000 in annual dividends. It was claimed that once allowance was made for tax provision, Ford Sherington's true earning rate approached thirty-five per cent on ordinary capital. An article from *The 'Wild Cat' Monthly* summarised:

> As an investment medium, Ford Sherington is comparatively unknown, all the more so because its scrip pays only random visits to the Sydney 'Change. Its products are, however, well known indeed – travel goods carrying the Fordite and Regal label, and including the old schooldays friend, the Globite school-case.
>
> Although de-centralisation of manufacture at first glance appears extreme for such a modestly capitalised organisation, transport is a major difficulty where goods of this nature are concerned.[102]

In 1963, repayment of the existing preference share capital was effected, with the preference shareholders receiving 25/- a share. The Sherington family still held most of the ordinary shares except that Ray Moore as chairman of the Board had now acquired a significant holding. By the 1970s he was one of the most significant businessmen in Sydney, being represented on the boards of at least sixteen companies including Ansett Transport, Australian Gypsum Industries, Penfolds, as well as Ford Sherington. His management style was said to be 'leaning towards financial conservatism – high levels of working capital, relatively little borrowing, and a general tendency towards self-financing'.[103]

Some new directions for Ford Sherington began to take shape. In the late 1950s, Frank Sherington came on as secretary of the company, while Bruce Sherington, son of the managing director Bill Sherington, also joined the company and board.

---

102 'Ford Sherington Holdings Ltd', *The 'Wild Cat' Monthly*, 7 February 1959.
103 'The Raymont Companies', *Share Market*, 1972.

Bruce in particular was anxious for the company to move into manufacturing new products. The staple product was the Globite suitcase for school and other uses, but there was also the emergence of tourism and both sea and air travel, growing on a mass scale. This led to production of more 'luxury' items such as the leather 'Regal' suitcase.

While such discussions were occurring, Marjorie, the wife of Bill Sherington, still the managing director of Ford Sherington, died in February 1964. As in 1928, family life affected company affairs. Many were aware that Bill Sherington's former energy for company affairs was now deeply affected. Nevertheless, in 1965 it was decided to move the factory to the south-western suburb of Kingsgrove as part of the proposed modernisation of manufacture. The new factory cost about $440 000, while the Kippax Street factory had a prospective value of about $330 000. The move itself allowed the creation of new ventures. In 1968–69, the company developed a moulded school case still under the brand name Globite. In 1969 a small investment was made in an associated company for car seats for children, a product designed to meet the emerging focus on road safety standards. In particular, with a growing road toll there was a move towards safety belts in cars and specifically provision for babies in capsules and then children in special forms of child restraint seats.[104]

Threats to the new directions of Ford Sherington now arose not from internal company disputes, as in the 1920s, but from changes to local capital markets. The growth of the share market in the 1960s, stimulated in part by the mining boom, led to financiers casting their eyes over the balance sheets of well-managed but conservatively financed enterprises. In February 1970, a financial report in the local *Daily Mirror* (which had been long produced in Kippax Street near to the old Ford Sherington building) reviewed the future of the company. The report noted that while company growth had been slow there were prospects for

104 Ford Sherington Documents.

expansion. It was expected that the company would step up production to meet the increasing demand from tourism and also for the range of school cases. While there had been two bonus share issues since the formation of the public company in 1950, share sales 'on the market' remained rare. The company had a strong cash flow that had financed both the new factory and new assets. While it was noted that its strong asset base made possible a takeover offer, it was expected that the strong share holdings in the Sherington family would provide resistance. The strong asset backing meant the board could consider such strategies as a further bonus share issue that would make a potential takeover expensive.[105]

Within two years, takeover proceedings were in place, not from a rival manufacturer but from the property developer and Hungarian-born migrant Paul Strasser under his firm Revere Developments. The great attraction was the estimated value of all the properties which Ford Sherington now held including Kingsgrove, Kippax Street, a factory in Brisbane and the factory in Port Elizabeth, South Africa, the latter of which had been sold or were in the process of being sold, so adding to the liquid assets of the company. On this basis Paul Strasser made an offer of $2.60 per share which some estimated was still below the value of the company but was double the share price at the time. According to one report 'Ford Sherington was a takeover plum moulded by that greatest of takeover plums – Raymont Moore'.[106]

An astute chairman who had been involved with Ford Sherington for four decades, Ray Moore had also held a large parcel of shares in the company. His prospective decision to sell his shares in a company he had guided for so long was a crucial moment in the history of the company.

The members of the Sherington family were still the major shareholders, but many probably had little option but to sell.

105 Ibid.
106 *Jobsons*, 18 August 1972.

Apart from Bruce Sherington, most Sheringtons in the company were near to retirement age or were not in good enough health to mount a rearguard campaign. Many had much of their capital tied up in the company. Some needed the funds. As one example, Dorothy Chambers, sister of Bill Sherington, had been widowed for over a decade, and although a canny investor had reached a period of her life where she needed capital. Bruce Sherington, however, did try to see if negotiations could take place for mergers with other travel goods manufacturers. The situation was further complicated by the generally low state of the travel goods industry with the prospect of overseas competition and reduced tariffs which the new Whitlam Government would soon introduce. In effect, a takeover seemed the only viable option.

The takeover was still a great blow to Bill Sherington who had spent more than forty years as managing director of a company which he had joined reluctantly on the eve of the 1930s Depression. In this sense, the company had become his family duty rather than his wish in life. At the end of July 1972, he wrote to his son Bruce in what was to be virtually the last testament for Ford Sherington:

> I am sorry that we have come to the parting of the ways with our shareholders and transfer to such people as Revere. However on full review it is hard to see that we could avoid it . . . The price of $2.60 is an attractive one for most if not all shareholders and we should not deny people rights of acceptance. I see the Sheringtons hold 26% of the capital and I think over the next ten years there could be more fragmentation of holdings . . . This does not overcome the fact that it is a sad fact so soon after my retirement and your drive and energy action in the firm. I hope everything is tied up for the staff and you do not leave before careful thought.[107]

107 Letter, 'Dad' to 'Bruce', 31 July 1972.

The family venture and enterprise that had begun in the 1890s was now almost over. Bruce Sherington decided not to stay with Ford Sherington despite the overtures of Sir Paul Strasser and others that he remain. Within six months Ford Sherington was incorporated into the extensive business empire of Strasser. His own family owned company of Parkes Developments had shareholders' funds of $12.7 million. Much of his wealth came from net increases in property assets most of it supported through borrowings, the very antithesis of the management of Ford Sherington.[108] Over the next two years the Strasser empire dissolved crushed by the national credit squeeze of 1974–75. The assets of Ford Sherington and other acquisitions were distributed.

A quarter of a century later an entrepreneur outside the Sherington family tried to revive the Globite trademark through manufacture in China. But Globite now seemed more part of a memory of an age past than a global product for the future. At the 2000 Sydney Olympics, those attending the opening ceremony received a plastic replica of a Globite school case. What was once a family business enterprise had turned into a national cultural icon.

By the end of the twentieth century the first generation of Sheringtons born in Australian had all died. In the early twenty-first century, one hundred and twenty-five years after the arrival of Ada Caroline and her three sons in Brisbane in 1889, the second generation of Australian-born members of the Sherington family had children and even grandchildren. Those named Sherington and those descended from the extended Sherington family are now part of a wide network that has spread across the continent even with a number of global contacts. And the nature of locality has been transformed as much as the idea of enterprise. In place of farming in Westleton, retail in South London and manufacturing in Sydney, the enterprise of individual members of the extended Sherington family has been and is in

108 *The National Times*, 11–16 December 1972.

such areas as property development, building construction and hardware, banking, IT, marketing, and mining as well as such professions as engineering, medicine, law and physiotherapy and the academic study of history. And yet the history of a family and its name still remains a prime way of how we come to understand and frame our own identities. In this way we can still try to understand our ancestors even if their lives seem to be now part of a world so different from our own.

A catalogue of Alfred Ford trunks, boxes and baths, c.1890.

A gathering of Ford Sherington employees, c.1910. Seated in the front row on the left is Ada Caroline Sherington; three seats from her is her son Guy who sits two seats from Alfred Ford and his wife Clara, who is next to her nephew William Henry Sherington and his wife Mabel.

Mabel Helen Oxby on her wedding day 1904.

Alfred Ford company in Elizabeth Street, c.1907.

The Oxby family from New Zealand. Back row from left to right: Mary and Bill Oxby. Middle row from left to right: Annie, Fred, Emily (the mother) and Lottie Oxby. Front row from left to right: Mabel and Sid Oxby.

Ford Sherington factory in Kippax Street, Surry Hills, c.1912.

Back row, second from the left: Major Guy Sherington as part of the AIF Headquarters staff, c.1917.

Children of William Henry and Mabel Helen Sherington, c.1919. Seated at the front is eleven-year-old William; in the middle row from left to right is six-year-old Frank, ten-year-old Dorothy, and six-year-old Charles; at the back is three-year-old Don.

William Henry and Mabel Helen Sherington and family c.1916. From the left: Frank, William Henry, William George, Marjorie, Charles, Mabel Helen with Donald, and Dorothy.

A 1920s picnic at Bowral. From the left: Frank, Ada, Charles, Donald, Mabel Helen, Dorothy, and William Henry. The family Overland Tourer stands behind.

The showroom in the Brisbane Ford Sherington factory, 1959.

The new Ford Sherington factory at Kingsgrove, c.1967.

A 1963 reunion for brother and sister Sid Oxby and Mabel Sherington, seated at far right of the table. Sid's son Les and his wife Molly stand second and third from right. Mabel's son Bill and daughter Ada stand fourth and fifth from left. Bill's wife Marjorie stands far right.

'Bramhall', Britannia St, Pennant Hills.

A gathering of cousins, Melbourne 2010. Standing left to right: Geoffrey Sherington, Malcolm Chambers, Don Sherington, and Grant Sherington. Seated left to right: Kay Wilson, Elizabeth Sharpe, Barbara Dawson, Annette Kendall.

And so in the end is a beginning: the graveyard of St Peter's, Westleton, turned into a wildlife sanctuary.

Appendix I
Family Line of Descent

Sherington family, male line of descent.

Christian name	Place of birth	Year of birth	Year of death	Age at death	Occupation	Wife's maiden name
Thomas	Westleton?	1500?	1552	52?	yeoman	Margery
William	Westleton	1530	1595	65	yeoman	Joanne
Thomas	Westleton	1569	1638	69	yeoman	Temperance
William	Westleton	1603	1666	63	yeoman	Ann
William	Westleton	1648	1719	69	yeoman	(Mrs) Martha Knapp
William	Westleton	1690	1752	62	'gentleman'	Hannah Tink
John	Westleton	1737	1816	79	farmer	Ann Reeve

Christian name	**Place of birth**	**Year of birth**	**Year of death**	**Age at death**	**Occupation**	**Wife's maiden name**
Henry	Yoxford	1776	1852	76	hairdresser	Charlotte Winter
Charles	Wickham Market	1814	1868	54	hairdresser	Mary Cottom
William	Norwood	1843	1897	54	trade	Ada Banfield
William	Dulwich	1874	1927	53	manufacturer	Mabel Oxby

Appendix II
Family Biographies

The biographies from the sixteenth century to the early nineteenth century are based principally on parish registers and wills. As such they refer to dates of baptisms and burials as recorded in the parish registers. The biographies from the mid-nineteenth century rely on national records and registration of marriages, birth and deaths as well as on census information and personal correspondence.

Thomas Sherington (c.1500–1552)

Thomas Sherington was a yeoman (a farmer of a large amount of land) and the first of the Sherington family known to have been associated with the village of Westleton on the east coast of Suffolk. He may have been born in Westleton but more likely he came from Norfolk, although there is a suggestion that he carried an alias of the family name of Cudon which had been long attached to the ancient port of Dunwich in close proximity to Westleton. He grew up in the reign of Henry VIII when there was much profit making in buying and selling rural land. Thomas was formally admitted to his land holdings at a manorial court in 1536, a process dating from the medieval period. This could suggest that by then he was already resident in Westleton. When Thomas died he left sizeable land holdings in Westleton. After making some provision in his will of 1551 for his wife Margery during her lifetime, the lands of Thomas went to his eldest son John but with proviso for support of his second son William and William's two daughters Margery (Marjorie) and Battye (Beatrice). Robert, another son of Thomas, had been buried in 1545 and thus does not appear in Thomas' will.

Thomas' eldest son John became the wealthiest man in Westleton, marrying in 1571 Joane Bury of the village of Worlingham in Suffolk. They had a son John baptised in 1572 and a daughter named Jeromine baptised in 1577. John and Joanne's son John then had a son named John baptised in 1597 and a daughter named Elizabeth baptised in 1599. The parish registers then give no further indication of the future of John Sherington's descendants. The main line of male descent in Westleton passed from Thomas to the second son William as indicated below.

The daughters of Thomas and Margery married into other families of some note. Elizabeth married John Jaye at Westleton in 1546. John Jaye was also mentioned in her father Thomas's will. In 1558, after Thomas had died, his daughter Marjorie married Robert Reeve who was probably associated with the well-known Reeve family in the nearby village of Yoxford.

William Sherington (1530–1595)

Born in Westleton, William Sherington was the second son of Thomas (above). He grew up in the last years of Henry VIII and the turbulence of Edward VI and Mary but most of his adult life was in the reign of Queen Elizabeth I.

William and his wife Joane had eleven children, of whom seven seemed to have survived beyond childhood. In birth order they were Margerye (baptised and buried 1568), Thomas (baptised 1569), Elizabeth (baptised 1571 and buried 1583), William (baptised 1573), Luke (baptised 1587), Francet (baptised 1575 and buried 1576), Robert (baptised 1577), Rafe (baptised 1580), Samuel (baptised 1581), Priscilla (baptised and buried 1583) and Joane (baptised 1584).

In his will of 1595, William left his house and all his lands to his wife Joane, with the property reverting after two years to his eldest son Thomas. There was also a proviso that the other surviving children – William, Robert, Samuel, Luke and Joane – would receive sums of money. (It was the pattern of primogeniture that allowed the eldest son to inherit but made some provision for younger children including daughters. This seems to have continued for future generations of Sheringtons in Westleton).

The biography of William's eldest son Thomas is outlined below. Of the other children of William Sherington, his second son, also named William, married Joan Dennet in Westleton in 1596. William and Joan had two sons – Robert (baptised 1599) and William (baptised 1603). William himself died in 1627. The Sherington family had begun to spread beyond Westleton from this period onwards. Robert Sherington, son of William, married twice – Joan of Westleton and then then Mary Eade from Leiston in Suffolk in 1625. Eventually Robert Sherington's descendants helped establish a line of the family in Lowestoft, on the Suffolk border with Norfolk and then in Yarmouth across the border. However, it would seem that both lines of the Sherington family maintained contact for many years as the baptisms and deaths of Robert Sherington and his children were recorded in the Westleton parish registers until at least the mid-1600s, suggesting that they retained land and even residence in Westleton up to the mid-seventeenth century.

Thomas Sherington (1569–1638)

Thomas was born in Westleton as the eldest son of William (above). Thomas carried the first name of his grandfather who was the founder of the family dynasty in Westleton. Thomas was married to Temperance. According to the parish registers, in a period of twenty-four years they had nine children of whom seven survived childhood: Ann (baptised and buried 1599), Thomas (baptised 1600), William (baptised 1603), Francis (baptised 1606), Temperance (baptised and buried 1608), Robert (baptised 1610), Elizabeth (baptised 1614), John (baptised 1617) and Mary (baptised 1623).

In his will written in 1637 the year before his death but proved at Yoxford in May 1638, Thomas left his wife Temperance a number of personal items but little else. He left 'all my lands and [tenements] . . . which I had by inheritance from my father' to his eldest son, also named Thomas, who was then required to pay to four other surviving adult children, William, Robert, John and Elizabeth, a total sum of twenty pounds following the death of their mother Temperance. Such payments were to take place at the 'Westleton church porch' perhaps signifying a village tradition. Each of these four children would also receive a 'pictle' of land. The will also made provision for his daughter Frances who had married John Crispe of Westleton. She would receive twenty shillings (each year) from the rent of the 'Lampetts' ('Lamb Pits') which her father Thomas had bought. There was also provision to pay his son John (aged twenty in 1537) five pounds when he finished his apprenticeship. And to his will 'Thomas Sheringtonn' left not his signature but his mark, indicating that he was not fully literate.

Aged in his late thirties, Thomas, who inherited most of the family lands, died childless in 1638, the same year as his father. The family lands reverted to the second-born child, William, who was three years younger than his brother.

William Sherington (1603–1666)

William was the son of Thomas (above), born in Westleton during the year that James I succeeded to the throne. He died when Charles II had been restored to the throne. He inherited the family lands when his brother Thomas died in 1638 without children. Politically and socially his life was marked by some trauma, including the English civil war and execution of Charles I followed by the rise of Cromwell. He was married to Anne who was possibly also from Westleton. The parish registers indicate that William and Anne had at least three children: William (baptised 1641, possibly died soon after), Anne (baptised 1643), and William (baptised 1648).

In 1669, three years after his death, William's widow Anne and a Thomas Bale of the village of Brampton (which is on the way to Lowestoft on the border with Norfolk) entered into a bond of £310 pounds (then a considerable sum) to administer the estate of William Sherington. This suggests that the family estate was then of substantial wealth.

William Sherington (1648–1718)

Son of William Sherington (above), William was born in Westleton. He lived through the period of the Commonwealth under Cromwell, the restoration of Charles II and the reigns of James II, William and Mary and Anne. In Suffolk, as elsewhere in England, this was a time of some political and social turmoil but many yeomen and gentry did well.

In 1690 William married Mrs Martha Knapp who would have been a widow, although both were described as 'single persons' in the parish registers, William and Hannah had two children recorded in the parish registers: William (baptised 1690) and Robert (baptised 1693). In 1719, the first-born son of William, entered into a bond with a Robert Bacon of the nearby village of Kelshall and John King of the village of Halesworth in north-east Suffolk, to administer the estate of William Sherington in a mode similar to that in which his mother had administered the estate of his father's, as noted above.

William Sherington (1690–1752)

Son of William Sherington (above), he was born in Westleton. William lived most of his adult life in the Hanoverian ascendancy of the reigns of George I and George II. In contrast to the political and religious troubles of the seventeenth century, this was a period of prosperity and economic growth in Suffolk. We know that William Sherington married Hannah Tink, but there is no clear indication in the parish registers as to when they married. The parish registers do indicate that they had the following children: William (baptised 1721), John (buried 1738), Robert (baptised 1735), John (baptised 1737) and Thomas (baptised 1741). In some of these parish entries William is described as 'Mr'or even 'Gent'.

In his will and last testament written in 1747, five years before his death, William described himself as a 'gentleman', a term then in common use for those once regarded as just wealthy yeomen. In his will he made extensive provision for his wife and his family. For her lifetime his 'dear' wife Hannah would occupy his cottage and would receive an annual sum of five pounds. His first-born son William, aged twenty-six in 1747, inherited most of the family extensive landholdings in Westleton and surrounding area, including annuities from tenements. To his second-born son Robert (aged only twelve when the will was written) as well as to John (aged ten) and Thomas (aged six), he provided an annual annuity of five pounds each until they reached the 'majority age' of twenty-one. In apparent accord with family or Westleton tradition (as seen above in Thomas Sherington's will of 1638), the annuities to Hannah and the three brothers would be paid half-yearly on the 'Feast Day of Saint Michael the Archangel' and the day of 'Administration of our Blessed Lady Mary the Virgin'. Once they attained the age of twenty-one, Robert, John and Thomas were to receive an endowment of sixty pounds. As the eldest son and chief beneficiary under the will, William was required to ensure that if necessary his brothers were apprenticed to a trade. Second-born son Robert would inherit the family cottage when his mother died and third-born son John would be given a cottage and yard on turning twenty-one. (There were no similar provisions for the youngest brother Thomas). Overall, the will granted most but not all the family inheritance to William the eldest son who had to assume some responsibility for his younger brothers. The estate was now large enough to provide some security for all the family members.

The death of William the 'gentleman' probably marked the high point of the Sherington family fortunes in Westleton. But signs of almost three centuries of Sheringtons in Westleton still remained. The twin gravestone of William and Hannah survives amidst the wild heathland in St Peter's graveyard, Westleton. And the descendants of William and Hannah's son Robert seemed to have remained in the area if not the village of Westleton until well into the nineteenth century.

John Sherington (1737–1816)

John was born in Westleton, the third surviving son of William and Hannah (above). In April 1760, the last year of the reign of George II, he married twenty-year-old Ann Reeve from the village of Yoxford (Ann was probably from the same family into which Marjorie Sherington had married two centuries earlier). John and Ann were wed under the Marriage Act of 1753 which required that 'banns' be read aloud announcing the prospective marriage on the three Sundays before the wedding, and in the home parish of each partner. Once wed John and Ann lived in

Yoxford. Parish and other records suggest that between 1762 and 1785 John and Ann had twelve children of whom nine survived childhood, with a number of twin births: John (baptised and buried 1762), William (baptised and buried 1762), William (baptised 1765), John (baptised 1765), Maria (baptised 1767), Elizabeth (baptised 1767), Thomas (baptised 1768), Sarah (baptised 1771), Henry (baptised 1776), Robert (baptised 1776), James (baptised 1780) and Ann (baptised 1785). John was the last of the Westleton Sherington line of direct male descent to live his entire life in Suffolk.

Henry Sherington (1776–1852)

A younger son of John and Ann Sherington, Henry was born in Yoxford during the year of the American Revolution. Henry was the first Sherington in three centuries, in this direct line of male descent, to move beyond the boundaries of Suffolk (his twin brother Robert may have moved to London as records show he died in Wandsworth in 1848; his younger brother James remained in Yoxford, married and had eight children). In 1805 Henry Sherington married Charlotte Winter from the nearby village of Cookley where there had once been Sibton Abbey the landlord for parts of Westleton. The couple soon moved to Wickham Market in central Suffolk. Here they had seven children of whom all but three seem to have survived infancy: Robert (baptised 1806 and buried 1807), Robert (baptised 1807), Matilda (baptised 1810 but probably died in infancy), Sarah (baptised 1812 but possibly died the same year), Sarah (baptised 1813) and Charles (baptised 1814). All these children were baptised in the Church of England. Two later-born children were baptised in the Methodist chapel as part of the of the Methodist 'district circuit' of Framlingham and Peasenhall (a village close to Yoxford in Suffolk): Charlotte (baptised 1816) and Betsy (baptised 1824). By the 1830s Henry and his family had moved to Norwood in South

London where Henry practised his trade as a 'hairdresser' in the manner of his brother James still in Yoxford. He died in Lambton Surrey after a life journey of change in locality, occupation and religious affiliation.

Charles Sherington (1814–1868)

Charles was the youngest son of Henry and Charlotte (above). Born in Suffolk, he spent all his adult life in Norwood, South London. Of 'independent means', he seems to have built a business on his declared occupation of 'hairdresser'. He married Mary Cottom at Lambeth in 1842. They had five children: William Charles (born 1843), Mary (born 1848), Ann (born 1849) and Helen (born 1853) and Charles (born 1855). A man of firm religious attachments, he was associated with the chapel across the road from his residence of Codrington Villa in High Street Norwood. He was buried in West Norwood cemetery with some ceremony but his grave site cannot now be found.

William Charles Sherington (1843–1897)

Born in Norwood, William Charles was the eldest child of Charles and Mary Sherington. In the 1860s he formed a close friendship with the Ipswich corset manufacturer William Pretty who would marry Ann Sherington, one of William Charles' sisters. William Charles was born in the same year as William Pretty but he had none of Pretty's business and entrepreneurial skills. In 1873 he married Ada Caroline Banfield who was a friend of his sister Ann. They had three sons: William Henry (born 1874), Charles Arthur (born 1876) and John Guy (born 1880). In 1880 Ada Caroline divorced him on the grounds of cruelty. William Charles left London in the 1880s and migrated to America where he was later caught up in the events surrounding the murder of his sister Helen at Middletown near San Francisco in 1890. He apparently died in San Francisco in 1897.

Ada Caroline (Banfield) Sherington (1852–1936)

Born in West London, Ada Caroline was the eldest daughter of Henry Banfield, a china dealer from Somerset and his wife Jane. Ada became involved with the Sherington family when the Banfields moved from West London to the Crystal Palace area in the 1860s. After her divorce from William Charles Sherington, Ada and her sisters Clara and Alice migrated to Australia along with her three sons, settling first in Brisbane and then Sydney. With guidance and financial assistance from William Pretty and other members of the Pretty family, she established a new successful business for her three sons which eventually became Ford Sherington.

William Henry Sherington (1874–1927)

Born in London, William Henry was the eldest son of William Charles and Ada Caroline Sherington. He played a major role in establishing a business relationship with Alfred Ford in the 1890s, leading to the formation of Ford Sherington in Australia in 1910. In 1904 he married Mabel Helen Oxby from New Zealand but of Essex background. They had seven children: Mabel Ada (born 1905), William George (born 1907), Dorothy Emily (born 1909), Marjorie Clara (born 1911 and died 1922), Frank Henry (born 1913), Charles Alfred (born 1913) and Donald Saville (born 1916). From 1924 the family lived at Pennant Hills. Mabel outlived her husband by more than forty years moving with her daughter Ada to Epping in the 1950s.

Charles Arthur Sherington (1876–1938)

Arthur was the second son of William Charles and Ada Caroline Sherington. He maintained close relations with the Pretty family in Suffolk. He served in the First World War and then married Olive Hingley in England before his return from the war. Arthur played little part in the postwar affairs of Ford Sherington but he and Olive continued contacts with the Prettys, particularly with Frank, the son of William Pretty. He was groomsman at Frank and Edith Pretty's wedding. His wife Olive was present at the Sutton Hoo archaeological dig in 1939.

John Guy Sherington (1880–1928)

Guy was the third son of William Charles and Ada Caroline Sherington. He achieved prominence in the Sydney business community before the First World War. He served in the war, receiving the award of Officer of the British Empire for helping to organise plans for the return of Australian troops. He married Beatrice Antell after the war, before he returned to Australia. On coming back to the business in Australia, Guy quarrelled with his elder brother William over the future direction of Ford Sherington. William and Guy died within six months of each other, William in 1927 and Guy in 1928. Guy and Maud had two sons, Peter and Ian, in the early to mid-1920s.

Mabel Ada Sherington (1905–1966)

Ada was the eldest child of William Henry and Mabel Helen Sherington. Following the early death of her father she spent most of her life as her mother's companion.

William George Sherington (1907–1993)

William George was the eldest son of William Henry and Mabel Helen Sherington. He became managing director of Ford Sherington at the age of twenty-three and remained in the post for over forty years. In 1934 he married Marjorie Frances Sherington. They had four children: David (born 1935), Bruce (born 1937), Elizabeth (born 1939) and Geoffrey (born 1945).

Dorothy Emily (Chambers) Sherington (1909–1992)

Dorothy was the second daughter of William Henry and Mabel Helen Sherington. Dorothy married Alan Chambers who later became secretary of Concrete Industries. They had three children: Helen (1937), Malcolm (1941) and Barbara (1943). The family lived at Epping but following the early death of Alan, Dorothy moved to the Anglican Castle Hill Retirement Village.

Marjorie Clara Sherington (1911–1922)

Marjorie was the third daughter of William Henry and Mabel Helen Sherington. She died of kidney failure while the family was living at Bowral. A prize and medal in her memory is awarded each year at Bowral Public School.

Frank Henry Sherington (1913–1972)

Frank was one of the male twins of William Henry and Mabel Helen Sherington. On the outbreak of war in 1939 he enlisted in the Sixth Division Second AIF. He married Phyllis Duesbury of a well-known family from Derby, England. They had two daughters: Helen (born 1946) and Kay (born 1950). After the war he finished a degree in accounting and joined Ford Sherington.

Charles Alfred Sherington (1913–1991)

Charles was one of the male twins of William Henry and Mabel Helen Sherington. He married Nea Pearce in Sydney and then moved to Melbourne to become managing director of the Melbourne branch of Ford Sherington. Charles and Nea had three children: Richard (born 1940), Annette (born 1942) and Grant (born 1945).

Donald Saville Sherington (1916–1994)

Donald was the youngest child of William Henry and Mabel Helen Sherington. He served in New Guinea during the Second World War. After the war he went to South Africa to become managing director of a Ford Sherington branch in Port Elizabeth. In South Africa he married Edith Bolton. They had two children: Donald (born 1946) and Evelyn (born in 1951 but killed in a car accident in 1968). The family later returned to live in Western Australia.